W9-DJP-096

 Rand McNally
Concise Atlas
of Europe

D1469250

🅐 Rand McNally & Company
Chicago/New York/San Francisco

Contents

Mapping the World

Where in the world am I? Have you ever looked at a map to discover just where you are in the world? And why a map?

A map makes it possible to understand where we are in relation to other people and places. Without maps, our understanding of the world would be limited to what we can see. A map is the best way to communicate information about the earth's surface.

The most accurate model of the earth is a globe. However, a globe doesn't show much detail of the earth. Nor is a globe easy to store in a drawer or carry around in your pocket. A flat map can have many details and is easy to carry or store. And a map can show large areas on a single piece of paper, making it easy to compare cities, countries, and other places.

But how can the curved surface of the globe be transformed into a flat map? Cartographers have found the answer, called map projection.

Map Projections

Most maps contain lines that cross to form a grid. These lines are called parallels of latitude and meridians of longitude. (For a more detailed description of latitude and longitude, see the section "Using the Atlas.") Transforming the round earth into a flat surface is done by projecting this grid onto a simple shape, such as a cylinder, a cone, or a plane shaped like a disc. The surface is then flattened, and the transformation has taken

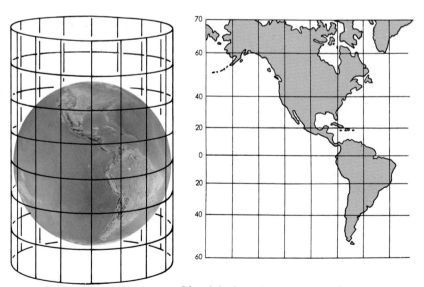

If a globe is projected onto a cylinder, it is called a cylindrical projection.

place. The round earth is on flat paper.

This is done in much the same way as a picture is projected onto a movie screen. Or think of a light inside a transparent globe, projecting the grid lines of the globe onto paper, where they can be traced.

However, each projection has some distortion. On a flat surface, it is impossible to represent the angles, distance, direction, and area that only a globe can faithfully show.

Experiment with this yourself. Peel an orange carefully and lay the orange peel on a flat surface. The peel will distort as you flatten it out.

While there is distortion in map projections, the places in the world are always in the right location on a map. The grid of latitude and longitude guarantees this accuracy.

There are many different kinds of map projections, and each is used to show specific features for a specific purpose. Often the type of projection is listed somewhere on the map. At the bottom of the physical-political maps and the environment maps in this atlas, the type of projection is stated.

But once the outline of the earth is on flat paper, how does the cartographer get information to fill in the map? One way is through satellite imagery.

Imagery and Maps

For thousands of years, people have been trying to get a bird's-eye view of the earth. At one time, they climbed trees or hills to get a better view of the terrain around them.

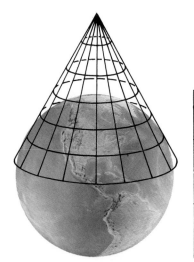

Projection of the globe onto a cone results in a conic projection.

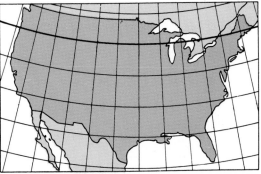

Modern technology has found a way for us to see more of our world than we can with the naked eye or a telescope. Today, there are satellites and airplanes circling the earth, equipped with cameras and electronic equipment acting as "remote sensors."

From a distance, remote sensors gather and record information about features on the earth. The cameras' sensitive film and the electronic instruments are so highly developed that they can detect things that our eyes cannot see. The pictures and information gathered by these satellites and airplanes are used by cartographers to create detailed, up-to-date maps.

Some of the best examples of remotely sensed imagery are the pictures gathered by the Landsat satellites. These satellites were launched in 1972, 1975, and 1978. As the Landsat satellites pass over the land taking pictures, information about water, soil, vege-tation, and crops is sent back to earth. Every eighteen days, each satellite orbits over the same area, so that changes in the terrain can be detected. As a result, the satellite images show changes in crop, vegetation, and farming patterns; damage resulting from hurricanes, earthquakes, floods, and fires; erosion patterns; desert sand movements; and other changes that make it necessary to update maps. In this way, technology provides mapmakers with the latest, most accurate information about the world.

Cartographers also make use of pictures taken by cameras mounted in aircraft. Very detailed maps can be produced from these high-altitude photographs, because all the roads and other features can be seen.

Because of advances in satellite technology and high-altitude photography, more details about the earth are constantly being discovered.

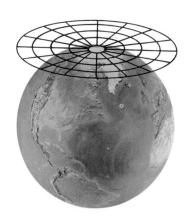
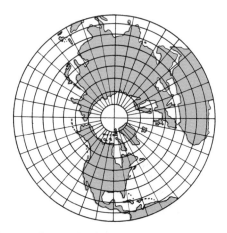

Plane-surface projection is based upon the projection of the globe onto a disc.

*An aircraft-mounted camera produced this high-altitude
photograph of the Goodland, Kansas, area.*

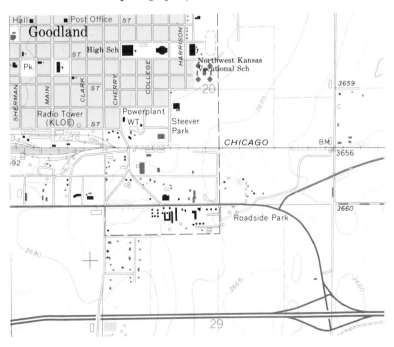

*Using the information on the high-altitude photograph,
cartographers made this detailed map of Goodland, Kansas.*

Geographic Features

Geographic Features

The study of geography is the study of the people and the land, and any feature found on the surface of the earth can be called a geographic feature. Geographic features are either natural or human-made. They are a result of natural or human activity.

About 5,000 million years ago, our planet came into existence. Millions of years passed, air and water developed, and the shaping of the earth's crust began. Continents collided, thrusting up mountains. Erupting volcanoes created islands. Glaciers passed over the land, depositing rocks and soil and leaving lakes in their wake. Water, wind, and sand cut away at rock.

Humans shaped the land in a different way. They cut down trees to plant crops for food. They blocked the rivers with dams and built reservoirs to bring water to dry land. Mountains are rugged and difficult to farm, so people settled mostly in the valleys and on the plains, where the soil was rich and easy to cultivate. They built cities along coastlines and rivers, because transportation routes were available there. Soon developments were found even in the deserts, where irrigation gave life to the dry land.

The drawing on the preceding page shows some of the different kinds of geographic features on the surface of the earth. It is easy to see the difference between the human-made and natural features. Humans mark the land with bold, even shapes, such as squares and triangles. Nature, however, is not so uniform, and mountains and rivers often cut a jagged line across the earth.

The following word list defines some of these land and water features.

altitude — Elevation or height above sea level.

archipelago — A group of islands.

atoll — A small island the shape of a ring or horseshoe.

bay — Part of a lake or sea that is partly surrounded by the shore land.

bayou — A slow, sluggish stream.

canyon — A deep, narrow valley having high, steep sides or cliffs.

cape — A narrow part of land that sticks out into the water along a shore.

coast — Land along the sea.

delta — Land made by soil that drops from a river at its mouth, the place where it meets a larger body of water.

desert — A large land area in which there is little or no rainfall. Few plants can grow on this dry land.

divide — The high land that separates two river basins. A river drains the water from land, and that land is its basin.

estuary — A narrow arm of the sea at the mouth of a river where the ocean tide meets the river current.

fjord — A deep, narrow inlet of the sea, between high, steep cliffs.

ford — A shallow place where a stream or body of water may be crossed by wading or driving through the water.

forest — A large area of land where many trees grow.

gorge — A narrow passage between steep mountains or hills; a steep rocky ravine.

gulf — A large area of the ocean or sea that lies within a curved coastline.

harbor — A sheltered body of water where ships anchor and are safe from the winds and waves of storms at sea.

hill — A small area of land that is higher than the land around it.

inlet — A small strip of water that reaches from a sea or lake into the shore land.

island — Land that is surrounded by water and smaller than a continent.

isthmus — A narrow piece of land that joins two larger bodies of land.

knoll— A small, round hill or mound.

lagoon — A pool of shallow water linked to the sea by an inlet.

lake — A body of water, usually fresh water, that is surrounded by land.

mesa — A flat topped, rocky hill with steeply sloping sides.

mountain — Land that rises very high, much higher than the land at its base. Mountains are much higher than hills.

mountain range — A row of mountains that are joined together. A mountain range makes a giant natural wall.

oasis — A place in a desert where people can get water. Water in an oasis comes from underground springs or from irrigation.

peninsula — A land area with a narrow link to a larger land area. It is almost surrounded by water.

plain — A large, flat land area.

plateau — A large land area that is high and generally very flat.

reef — A series of rocks in a body of water, the tops of which are slightly beneath or at the surface.

river — A large, moving body of fresh water that starts at a source in higher land.

sea — A large body of salt water nearly or partly surrounded by land. A sea is much smaller than an ocean.

snowline — The line on a mountain above which there is snow the year around.

sound — A long and wide body of water. A sound connects two larger bodies of water or separates an island from a larger body of land.

strait — A passageway of water that connects two large bodies of water.

tributary — A stream or small river that flows into another river or stream.

valley — The lower land between hills or mountains.

volcano — A cone-shaped mountain formed by lava and cinders, erupted thru a crater.

watershed — 1. The elevated land or divide separating two drainage areas. 2. The entire area drained by a river and its tributaries.

waves — A moving ridge of water which rises and falls.

whirlpool — Any place where water flows in a small circle.

Terrain

Europe Facts

Sixth largest continent
Second in population: 684,800,000
63 cities over 1 million population
Highest mountain: Elbrus, 18,510 feet
 (5,642 meters)
Most densely populated continent: 180 people
 per square mile (67 people per square
 kilometer)

URAL MOUNTAINS

Arctic Circle

SULA

Volga

SOVIET UNION
(EUROPEAN PORTION)

CENTRAL RUSSIAN UPLANDS

VOLGA PLATEAU

PRIVOLZSKAYA UPLAND

CASPIAN DEPRESSION

Dnepr

Don

CRIMEA PENINSULA

Black Sea

KEY

© 1979 Rand McNally & Co.

Many parts of Europe lie under the shadows of towering mountains. The most splendid of these peaks are the Alps. These shining pyramids of snow and stone are found in Switzerland, southeastern France, Austria, southern Germany, northern Italy, and northern Yugoslavia. The Alps make these countries a sightseer's paradise and a skier's adventureland.

Three major mountain systems flow out of the central mass of the Alps like tails from a kite. One of these tails, the Apennines, reaches south into the boot of Italy. Another, the Dinaric Alps, makes a jagged trail through Yugoslavia and Albania into Greece. The Third, the Carpathians, forms a graceful half-moon through Czechoslovakia and Romania.

Also reaching out from the Alps are many hills and plateaus. Nearly all of southern and central France is a wide upland, the Massif Central, that has been cut by rivers into hills. More hills ruffle parts of northern France and eastern Belgium — they are called the Ardennes Mountains, site of many fierce battles throughout history. Similar low hills and plateaus lie across southern Germany, in parts of Czechoslovakia, and in Austria.

Across the English Channel, Great Britain has a bumpy backbone known as the Pennine Chain of mountains. North of them are the famed Scottish Highlands, where long hillls covered with heather roll like frozen ocean waves across the countryside.

Northern mainland Europe is marked by mountains of another kind. The uplands of Norway and Sweden are bleak and barren, especially as they approach the white magnificence of the Arctic Circle. Huge glaciers once rumbled over the landscape, clawing deep grooves into the mountains. These grooves, flooded by the ocean, have become long waterways called fjords. The fjords at-

continued on page 15

Countries and Cities

Text on page 16

Arctic Circle

Arkhangelsk

RUSSIA

grad

Gor'kiy

Moscow ★ **SOVIET**   **UNION**
              (EUROPEAN   PORTION)   Kuybyshev

Kharkov

Volgograd

UKRAINE   Donetsk

Odessa

© 1979 Rand McNally & Co.

stanbul
EY

tract many tourists because of their awesome beauty.

Far to the east the Soviet Union's Ural Mountains mark the division between Europe and Asia. Such a mountain chain in the middle of a thousand-mile flatland is most unusual. The Urals are very old — formed about 225 million years ago. In that time they have worn down more and more.

Today the tallest of the Urals stands only a little more than six thousand feet (1,828.2 meters) above sea level, quite low in comparison with other major mountains.

Some of the most famous rivers in the world flow from Europe's mountains. Perhaps the best known is the Rhine, which rises in Switzerland and flows north past grape-clothed bluffs in Germany and France where the castles of medieval barons still scowl down on the river. Far longer than the Rhine is the fabled Danube River. It rises in Germany and drifts lazily in a southeasterly direction through seven nations and three capital cities before emptying into the Black Sea.

The north-central part of the continent is made up of the Great Northern European Plain. The huge region's rich farmlands supply food for much of Europe, and its many ores help to make the Ruhr Valley on the Rhine a world center for heavy industry. Food and machinery move out to the rest of Europe on a network of rivers connected by canals. The canals were dug by hand long ago in spillways, the natural trenches that were formed by the melting of the glacier twenty-five thousand years ago.

The Great Northern European Plain stretches from western France to nearly a thousand miles (1,609.3 kilometers) beyond Moscow, where it is broken at last by the rounded Urals. Here bustling Europe ends amid the lonely sweep of the wind through mountain forests.

Countries and Cities

In some ways Europe looks more like a jigsaw puzzle than a reasonable grouping of thirty-four nations. The boundaries of those countries — from the huge Soviet Union to tiny Luxembourg — were agreed upon only after much haggling through the centuries. In recent times, World Wars I and II caused boundary changes, and several new nations were formed as well.

The borders of most countries stop at mountains, rivers, or seas. When the first tribes migrated into an area, they usually chose a homeland that had some natural barrier where their warriors could defend them from attack. Today, many countries still are edged by such natural borders.

Cities tell us much about peoples of the past. Rome and Athens were known thousands of years ago, and the Roman Forum and Colosseum and the Acropolis and statues of Athens hint at life in ancient times. Paris dates back more than two thousand years. It was founded around 52 B.C. by Roman soldiers. Trondheim, in Norway, had its beginning around A.D. 998. Today it is the third largest city in Norway and an important export center. Clues in these and other cities hint at governments, religions, and pastimes of the people who once lived there.

The European continent averages 180 persons per square mile. Some of its countries, especially in the west, are among the most densely packed in the world. The Netherlands had 892 persons per square mile. But it is doing something few other countries are able to do — it is growing by reclaiming land from the sea.

Something a traveler moving through Europe notices is its many languages. Of the several dozen spoken, nearly all fall into three main groups.

The French, Italians, Spanish, Portuguese, and Romanians cannot understand one another. Nevertheless, all of their languages are based on the ancient Latin spoken by the Romans who once conquered those lands. These are the "Romance" languages.

The people of Germany, the Netherlands, England, Denmark, Sweden, and Norway speak six separate languages. Yet these, too, have their roots in a single language — the German of the tribes which occupied those areas in ages past.

To the east, the peoples of Poland, Czechoslovakia, Yugoslavia, Bulgaria, and Russia all speak languages based on the Slavic language of tribes that once lived there.

You might ask why an Italian doesn't understand a Spaniard, since their languages are alike. Or why the Germanic-speaking Dane doesn't understand the Germanic-speaking Briton. The answer lies in terrain, distance, and culture. Peoples of neighboring lands often were cut off from each other by natural barriers, or were separated by too many miles to meet often and talk. The Pyrenees closed Spain from France. A branch of the Alps shut off France from Italy. The North Sea separated the English from the Danes. And vast differences in cultures — life-styles — divided the Slavic-speaking Poles and the Russians. Each nation developed — over long ages — different ways of speaking what were once the same languages. In time the German of Germany was slightly different from that of the Netherlands. Across the North Sea the English people developed a distinct language using many German words, but also including words from Latin. And in the north, the Danes, Swedes, and Norwegians all used their own versions of the ancient German.

Today European languages are called Romance, Germanic, and Slavic. Only three major European countries do not fall into these groupings: Finland, Hungary, and Greece.

Each of the thirty-four nations of Europe has its own kind of government and a way of life that is unique to itself.

Animals

Most of the vast, animal-filled forests that once covered much of Europe were cut down long ago to make room for farms, cities, and towns. Many of Europe's animals were hunted for centuries, until they were wiped out. But in a few wild places still left — national parks, game preserves, and a few out-of-the-way places — some of the animals that once abounded in Europe can still be found.

A few of the shaggy, tusked boars that were the favorite game animal of medieval nobles still root in the underbrush of small forests in central Europe. Packs of wolves still howl in some places, and in the northern Soviet Union brown bears still lumber about. In the north of Sweden, Norway, Finland, and the western Soviet Union reindeer are herded like cattle by people of the northland, the Lapps.

In a protected forest of Poland about 1,600 wisents, the bisons of prehistoric Europe, live as they did many thousands of years ago—feeding in grassy clearings. Full grown, the animals stand six feet (1.82 meters) high at the shoulder.

Animals

Raven

Whimbrel

Brown Bear

Pine Marten

Wild Boar

Wolf

Griffon
Vulture

Roe Deer

Lesser
Spotted Eagle

Tur

Octopus

Conger Eel

In the Pyrenees Mountains between France and Spain lives the Pyrenean ibex, a mountain goat with curled horns. Another kind of mountain goat, the chamois, is found in the Alps.

Europe also has numerous small animals. Foxes, badgers, moles, rabbits, and squirrels are found in many places. Little, plump lemmings abound in the mountains of Norway and Sweden. The hedgehog is common in northern Europe and especially well-known in England. It has short, sharp "spikes" all over its back, like the quills of a porcupine only much thicker.

Small, striped wildcats prowl in parts of Yugoslavia and Bulgaria, and a rather large wildcat, the Spanish lynx, lives in Spain. It is three feet (0.91 meter) long with pointed ears and thick whiskers — a fast, fierce hunter.

Sparrows, thrushes, finches, nightingales, and ravens are found throughout central Europe. So are large birds of prey such as falcons and eagles. During the summer the big white stork is a common sight in cities of the Netherlands, Belgium, and Germany, where it nests on the chimneys of houses.

Various kinds of lizards and snakes, tortoises and turtles, frogs, toads, and salamanders are found in woodlands and meadows throughout Europe. Trout, salmon, and other fish swim in clear streams above the polluted areas. Many of the animal species found in Europe are also found on the North American continent.

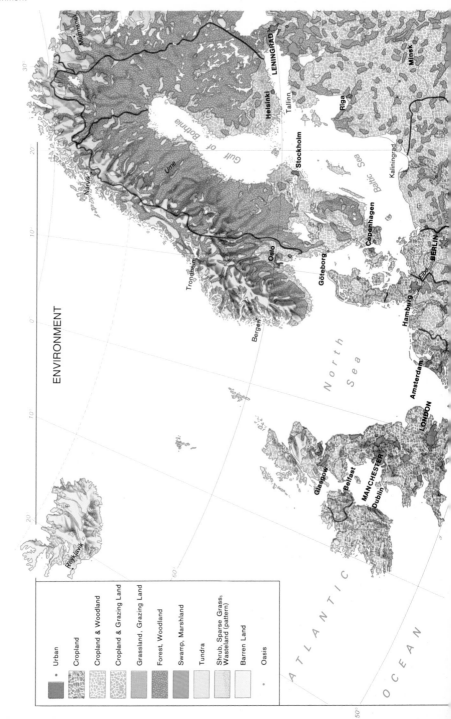

ENVIRONMENT

- Urban
- Cropland
- Cropland & Woodland
- Cropland & Grazing Land
- Grassland, Grazing Land
- Forest, Woodland
- Swamp, Marshland
- Tundra
- Shrub, Sparse Grass, Wasteland (pattern)
- Barren Land
- Oasis

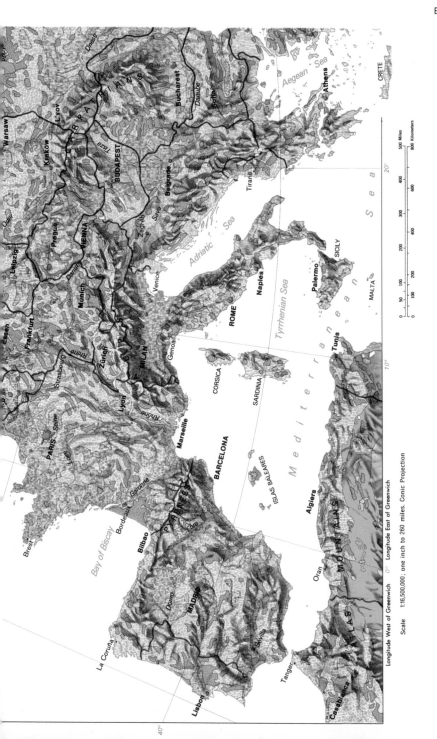

Longitude West of Greenwich   0°   Longitude East of Greenwich

Scale   1:16,500,000; one inch to 260 miles. Conic Projection

Scale 1:16 000 000; one inch to 250 miles. Conic Projection
Elevations and depressions are given in feet.

EUROPE LANGUAGES
BY
BOGDAN ZABORSKI

Scale 1:16,500,000; one inch to 260 miles Conic Projection

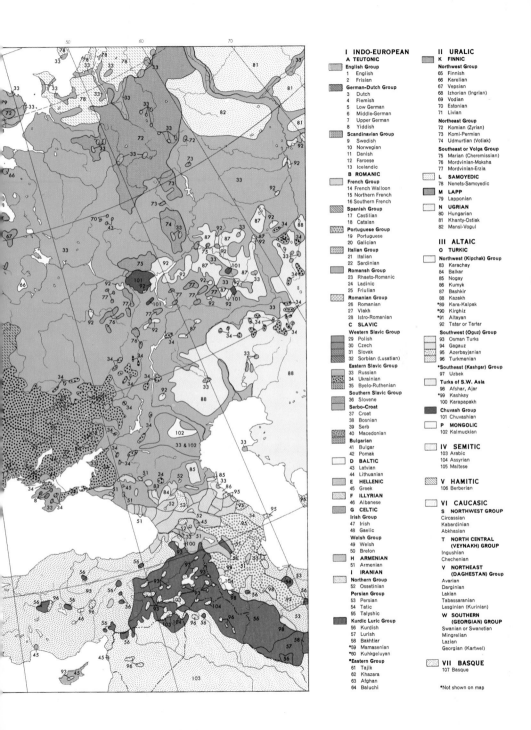

I INDO-EUROPEAN

A TEUTONIC

English Group
1 English
2 Frisian

German-Dutch Group
3 Dutch
4 Flemish
5 Low German
6 Middle-German
7 Upper German
8 Yiddish

Scandinavian Group
9 Swedish
10 Norwegian
11 Danish
12 Faroese
13 Icelandic

B ROMANIC

French Group
14 French Walloon
15 Northern French
16 Southern French

Spanish Group
17 Castilian
18 Catalan

Portuguese Group
19 Portuguese
20 Galician

Italian Group
21 Italian
22 Sardinian

Romansh Group
23 Rhaeto-Romanic
24 Ladinic
25 Friulian

Romanian Group
26 Romanian
27 Vlakh
28 Istro-Romanian

C SLAVIC

Western Slavic Group
29 Polish
30 Czech
31 Slovak
32 Sorbian (Lusatian)

Eastern Slavic Group
33 Russian
34 Ukrainian
35 Byelo-Ruthenian

Southern Slavic Group
36 Slovene

Serbo-Croat
37 Croat
38 Bosnian
39 Serb
40 Macedonian

Bulgarian
41 Bulgar
42 Pomak

D BALTIC
43 Latvian
44 Lithuanian

E HELLENIC
45 Greek

F ILLYRIAN
46 Albanese

G CELTIC

Irish Group
47 Irish
48 Gaelic

Welsh Group
49 Welsh
50 Breton

H ARMENIAN
51 Armenian

I IRANIAN

Northern Group
52 Ossetinian

Persian Group
53 Persian
54 Tatic
55 Talyshic

Kurdic Luric Group
56 Kurdish
57 Lurish
58 Bakhtiar
*59 Mamasenian
*60 Kuhkgeluyan

***Eastern Group**
61 Tajik
62 Khazara
63 Afghan
64 Baluchi

II URALIC

K FINNIC

Northwest Group
65 Finnish
66 Karelian
67 Vepsian
68 Izhorian (Ingrian)
69 Vodian
70 Estonian
71 Livian

Northeast Group
72 Komian (Zyrian)
73 Komi-Permian
74 Udmurtian (Votiak)

Southeast or Volga Group
75 Marian (Cheremissian)
76 Mordvinian-Moksha
77 Mordvinian-Erzia

L SAMOYEDIC
78 Nenets-Samoyedic

M LAPP
79 Lapponian

N UGRIAN
80 Hungarian
81 Khanty-Ostiak
82 Mansi-Vogul

III ALTAIC

O TURKIC

Northwest (Kipchak) Group
83 Karachay
84 Balkar
85 Nogay
86 Kumyk
87 Bashkir
88 Kazakh
*89 Kara-Kalpak
*90 Kirghiz
*91 Altayan
92 Tatar or Tarfar

Southwest (Oguz) Group
93 Osman Turks
94 Gagauz
95 Azerbayjanian
96 Turkmenian

***Southeast (Kashgar) Group**
97 Uzbek

Turks of S.W. Asia
98 Afshar, Ajar
*99 Kashkay
100 Karapapakh

Chuvash Group
101 Chuvashian

P MONGOLIC
102 Kalmuckian

IV SEMITIC
103 Arabic
104 Assyrian
105 Maltese

V HAMITIC
106 Berberian

VI CAUCASIC

S NORTHWEST GROUP
Circassian
Kabardinian
Abkhasian

T NORTH CENTRAL (VEYNAKH) GROUP
Ingushian
Chechenian

V NORTHEAST (DAGHESTAN) Group
Avarian
Darginian
Lakian
Tabassaranian
Lesginian (Kurinian)

W SOUTHERN (GEORGIAN) GROUP
Swanian or Swanetian
Mingrelian
Lazian
Georgian (Kartwel)

VII BASQUE
107 Basque

*Not shown on map

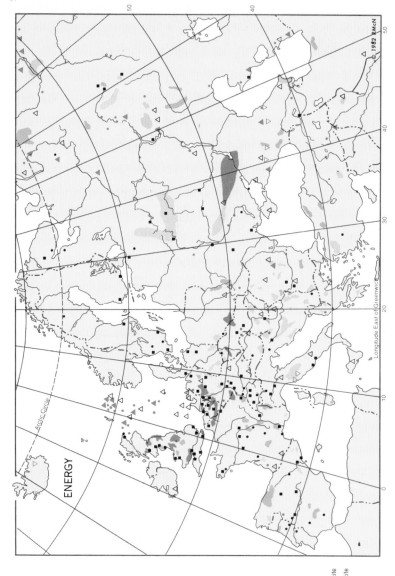

ENERGY

Energy Consumption
2,061,530 metric tons
coal equivalent-1982

HYDRO & NUCLEAR
ELECTRICITY-5%   FUELWOOD-1%
LIQUID 40%
GAS 18
SOLID 36

ENERGY

Energy Producing Plants

▷ Geothermal
• Hydroelectric
■ Nuclear

Mineral Fuel Deposits

• Uranium: major deposit
◁ Natural Gas: major field
• Petroleum: minor producing field
◁ Petroleum: minor producing field
◀ Petroleum: major producing field

Coal: major bituminous and anthracite
Coal: minor bituminous and anthracite
Coal: lignite

© 1982 RMcN
Longitude East of Greenwich
Arctic Circle

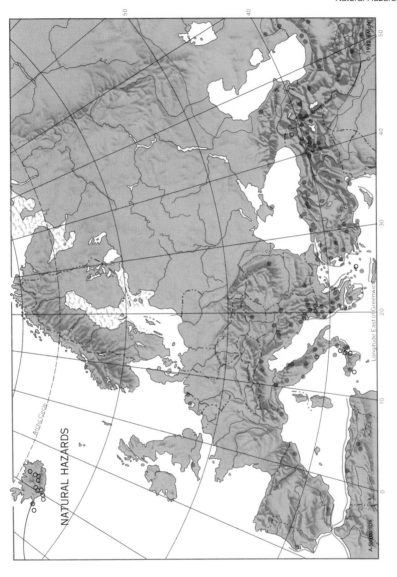

NATURAL HAZARDS

NATURAL HAZARDS

○	Volcanoes*
●	Earthquakes*
●	Major flood disasters*
|	Tsunamis
|	Limit of iceberg drift
	Temporary pack ice
	Areas subject to desertification
	*Twentieth Century occurrences

Arctic Circle

Longitude East of Greenwich

A-560000-1DS

© 1982 RM-N

Using the Atlas

An atlas is a guide to the world that can be used in many ways. You can look up places in the news and learn about the world. If you're interested in history, you can use an atlas to find famous towns and battle sites. You can even use an atlas to find the names of places in movies or to look up the lake you swam in last summer. But to discover the world with your atlas, you must be able to do five things:

1. Measure distances using a map scale
2. Use directions and latitude and longitude
3. Find places on the maps using letter-number keys
4. Use different kinds of maps
5. Use map symbols and legends

Figure 1

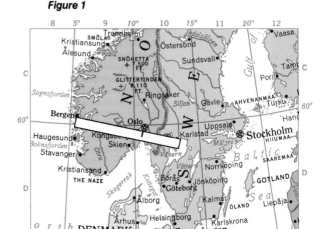

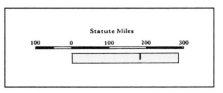

Figure 2

Measuring Distances

To understand a map, you must know its scale, or how large an area of the earth it shows. There are different types of map scales, but the bar scale is the easiest to use for determining distance.

For example, to find the distance between Bergen and Oslo in Norway, first you will find out how far Bergen is from Oslo on the map. Then by using a bar scale, you will learn what this means in actual distance on the earth.

1. Find Bergen and Oslo on the map in Figure 1.
2. Lay a slip of paper on the map so that

its edge touches the two cities. Move the paper so that one corner touches Bergen.

3. Mark the paper where it touches Oslo. The distance from the corner of this paper to the mark shows how far Oslo is from Bergen on the map.

4. The numbers in the map scale in Figure 2 show statute miles, or miles on the earth. Line up the edge of the paper along the map scale, putting the corner at 0.

5. Find the mark on the paper. The mark shows that Bergen is about 200 miles away from Oslo.

Using Directions and Latitude and Longitude

Most of the maps in this atlas are drawn so that north is at the top of the page, south is at the bottom, west is at the left, and east is at the right.

Many of the maps also have lines drawn across them — lines of latitude and longitude. These are lines drawn on a map or globe to make it easier to tell directions and to find places.

Lines of latitude are also called parallels of latitude. As shown in Figure 3, parallels run east and west, and they are numbered with degrees, which measure distance. One degree of latitude is about seventy miles (112.65 kilometers) long.

Latitude is measured as degrees north (N) or degrees south (S) of the equator. The equator was chosen as the dividing point because it marks the middle of the earth. It is at 0° latitude. The place farthest north on earth is the North Pole. It is located 90° north of the equator, or, simply, at 90° N. The South Pole is the earth's southernmost point, at 90° S.

You can use parallels of latitude to tell how far north or south a place is. For example, the map in Figure 1 shows that Bergen is north of the 60° parallel of latitude and Stockholm is south of it. So Bergen is farther north than Stockholm.

Lines of longitude are also called meridians. Figure 3 shows that meridians run north and south between the two poles. Like parallels, they are numbered with degrees.

But unlike parallels of latitude, meridians have no natural dividing line at which their numbering can begin. In the 1880s, an international conference solved this problem by selecting Greenwich, England, near London, to be the prime meridian, or 0° longitude. So, meridians measure how far east (E) or west (W) of Greenwich, England, a place is.

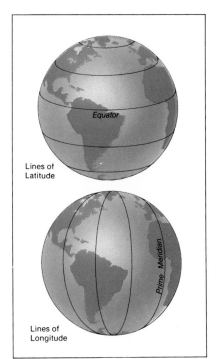

Figure 3

You can use the map in Figure 1 to find out which city is farther east, Bergen or Stockholm. Bergen is about 5° east of the prime meridian, or 5° E. Stockholm is about 20° E. This means that Stockholm is farther east than Bergen.

The east-west parallels and north-south meridians form a grid on a globe or map. You can find any place in the world by using latitude and longitude.

Finding Places

One of the most important things an atlas can do is tell you the location of a place — where it is. You may want to look up the city where a pen pal lives or find a town you're interested in visiting. To help you find places quickly and easily on a map, most atlases include an index of place-names with letter-number keys.

If you were studying South America, and read about Santiago, a city in Chile, here's how you would find it on a map:

1. Look up the city's name, Santiago, in the alphabetical index at the back of the atlas. (See Figure 4.) The number 31 is the page that the map is on. The letter-number key C2 is the guide to finding Santiago on the map on page 31. (See Figure 5.)

2. Turn to the map of southern South America on page 31. (See Figure 5.)

3. Find the letters **A** through **D** along the left-hand side of the map and the numbers **2** through **5** along the top edge of the map. These black letters and numbers are centered between the parallels of latitude and meridians of longitude.

Figure 4

San Juan, Puerto Rico	N18	77
San Salvador, Salvador	F7	76
Santa Fe, New Mexico	C5	74
Santiago, Chile	C2	31
Santo Domingo,		
Dominican Republic	E10	77
Sao Paulo, Brazil	A7	88

4. To find Santiago, use the letter-number key C2. Place your left index finger on C and your right index finger on 2. Move your left finger across the map and your right finger down the map, staying within the latitude and lon-

gitude grid lines on either side. Your fingers will meet in the box in which Santiago is located. (See Figure 5.)

You can use this method to find any place listed in the index of this atlas on the physical/political maps, pages 35-54.

Using Different Kinds of Maps

There are different kinds of maps, and each is especially suited for a certain topic. In this atlas, you'll find physical-political maps, physical maps, political maps, and thematic maps.

When people think of maps, they usually think of physical-political maps. The purpose of a physical-political map is to show the world's physical features and political units. Physical features include oceans, lakes, rivers, mountains, and other natural parts of the earth. Political units are states and countries and all the places they contain. These are human-made features.

Sometimes, the information on a physical-political map is separated to make two maps: a physical map, showing only natural features, and a political map, showing only human-made features.

Terrain maps use shaded relief to show the shape of the earth's surface. Shaded relief is a three-dimensional drawing of mountains and valleys on a map. Political maps show countries, major cities and roads.

A thematic map tells the story of a special topic, such as rainfall, population, trade, mineral resources, or any special aspect of the physical (natural) or political (human-made) environment.

Using Map Symbols and Legends

A symbol is something that stands for something else. In a way, a whole map is a symbol,

Figure 5　　　　　　　　　　　　　　　　　　Using the Atlas　**31**

South America, South/Physical-Political

because it represents the world or a part of it.

All the world's features — such as cities, rivers, and lakes — are represented with symbols on maps. Map symbols may be points, lines, or areas.

Point symbols are usually dots or stars. For example, the symbol for a city might be a dot, and the symbol for a state capital might be a star.

Line symbols are used for roads, rivers, or railroads. Often, rivers are shown with blue lines, and roads with black.

Area symbols show states, forests, deserts, or anything that covers a large area. On a map of the United States, for example, each state may be shown in a different color so that you can see where one state ends and the next state begins. Large areas of forest might be shown in green, and deserts could be a sand color. These different colors are area symbols.

A map legend explains the symbols used on the map. It is called a legend because it tells the story of the map. It is sometimes called a map key, because it unlocks the meaning of the map's symbols.

The environment map legend below divides the environment into ten major categories. If the area mapped has a city character with streets, factories, and buildings, it is shown as urban. If most of the area is farmland with crops, it falls into the cropland category. This legend should be used when reading the environment map in the book.

The physical-political map legend at the right divides the earth's geographic features into three major classes: cultural, land, and water features. Cultural features are human-made and include cities, roads, railroads, and boundaries. Land features are mountain peaks, mountain passes, and spot heights. (Spot heights tell the elevation of certain places on a mountain.) Water features are rivers, lakes, swamps, and any body of water. This legend should be used when working with the physical-political maps in the book.

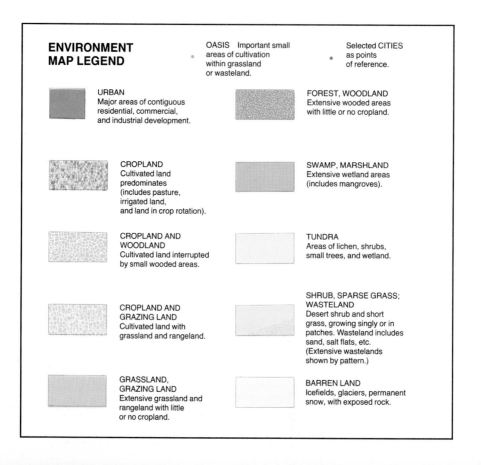

ENVIRONMENT MAP LEGEND

OASIS   Important small areas of cultivation within grassland or wasteland.

Selected CITIES as points of reference.

URBAN
Major areas of contiguous residential, commercial, and industrial development.

FOREST, WOODLAND
Extensive wooded areas with little or no cropland.

CROPLAND
Cultivated land predominates (includes pasture, irrigated land, and land in crop rotation).

SWAMP, MARSHLAND
Extensive wetland areas (includes mangroves).

CROPLAND AND WOODLAND
Cultivated land interrupted by small wooded areas.

TUNDRA
Areas of lichen, shrubs, small trees, and wetland.

CROPLAND AND GRAZING LAND
Cultivated land with grassland and rangeland.

SHRUB, SPARSE GRASS; WASTELAND
Desert shrub and short grass, growing singly or in patches. Wasteland includes sand, salt flats, etc. (Extensive wastelands shown by pattern.)

GRASSLAND, GRAZING LAND
Extensive grassland and rangeland with little or no cropland.

BARREN LAND
Icefields, glaciers, permanent snow, with exposed rock.

Map Symbols (Legend)
For maps on pages 34-54

CULTURAL FEATURES

Political Boundaries

━━━━━━━ International

┄┄┄┄┄┄ Secondary

Populated Places

Cities, towns, and villages

·····●● Symbol size represents population of the place

London
Bristol
York
Exeter
Yeovil

Type size represents relative Importance of the place

Major Urban Area

Area of continuous commercial, industrial, and resdential development in and around a major city

○ **Community within a city**

⊕ **Capital of major political unit**

☆ **Capital of secondary political unit**

LAND FEATURES

≈ **Passes**

+ 8,520 FT. **Point of elevation above sea level**

WATER FEATURES

Coastlines and Shorelines ─────────→

Indefinite or Unsurveyed Coastlines and Shorelines ─────────→

Lakes and Reservoirs ─────→

Canals ─────↓

Rivers and Streams ─────→

Falls and Rapids ─────→

Intermittent or Unsurveyed Rivers and Streams ─────→

Directional Flow Arrow ─────↗

Rocks, Shoals, and Reefs ─────────→

Miscellaneous

△ **Point of Interest**

∴ **Ruins**

Dam

Bridge

Dike

TYPE STYLES USED TO NAME FEATURES

EUROPE	Continent	*ALPS GLACIER*	Major Terrain Features
DENMARK	Country	MATTERHORN	Individual Mountain
BÉARN	Region, Province, or Historical Region	STROMBOLI KOLA PEN.	Island or Coastal Feature
PANTELLERIA (ITALY)	Country of which unit is a dependency in parentheses	*Ocean Lake River Canal*	Hydrographic Features
FED. REP. OF GER. (WEST GERMANY)	Alternate Name		
Rome (Roma)	Local or alternate city name		

Note: Size of type varies according to importance and available space. Letters for names of major features are spread across the extent of the feature.

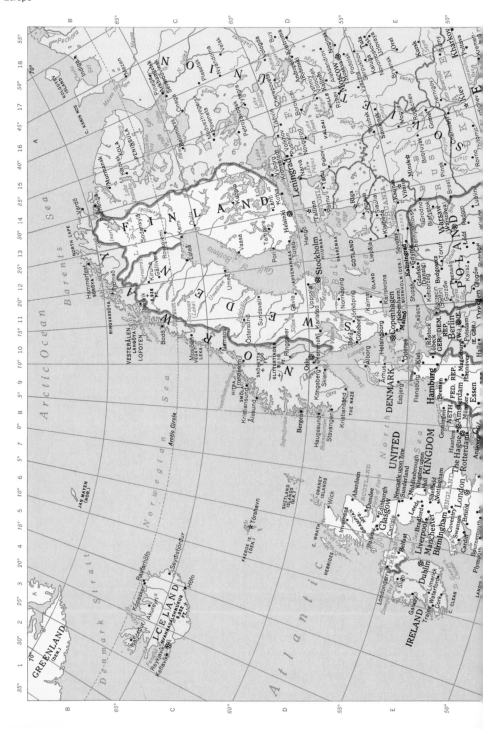

Statute Miles

Kilometers

Conic Projection

Longitude East of Greenwich

Longitude West of Greenwich

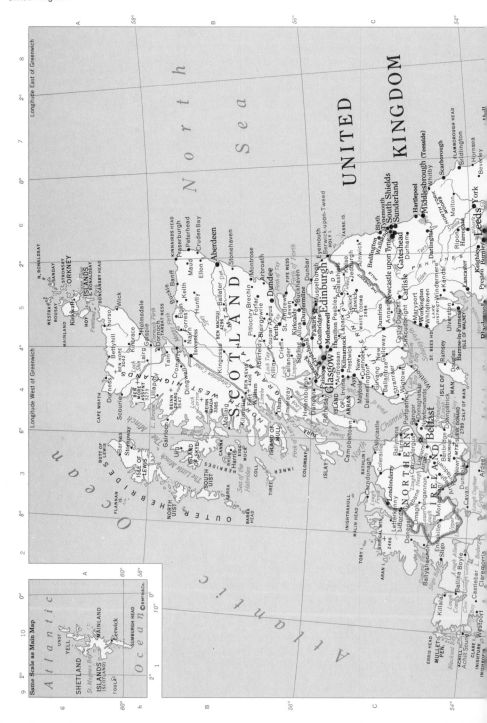

Longitude East of Greenwich

North Sea

UNITED

KINGDOM

SCOTLAND

Longitude West of Greenwich

ORKNEY ISLANDS

SHETLAND ISLANDS (SCOTLAND)

Ocean

Atlantic

OUTER HEBRIDES

Edinburgh

Glasgow

NORTHERN IRELAND

Belfast

Leeds

Middlesbrough (Teesside)

Same Scale as Main Map

SHETLAND ISLANDS (SCOTLAND)

MAINLAND

Lerwick

Atlantic Ocean

Conic Projection

Statute Miles

Kilometers

X-553600-21 -5-7-42

COSMO SERIES BRITISH MILES
Copyright by
RAND McNALLY & COMPANY
Made in U.S.A.

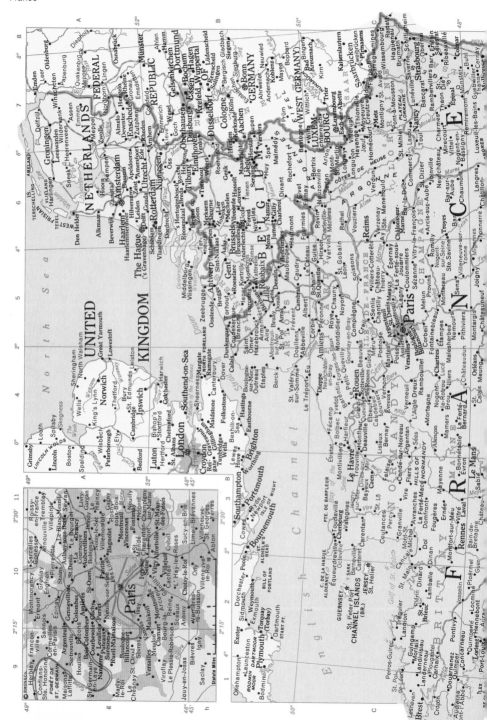

Conic Projection

Statute Miles
Kilometers

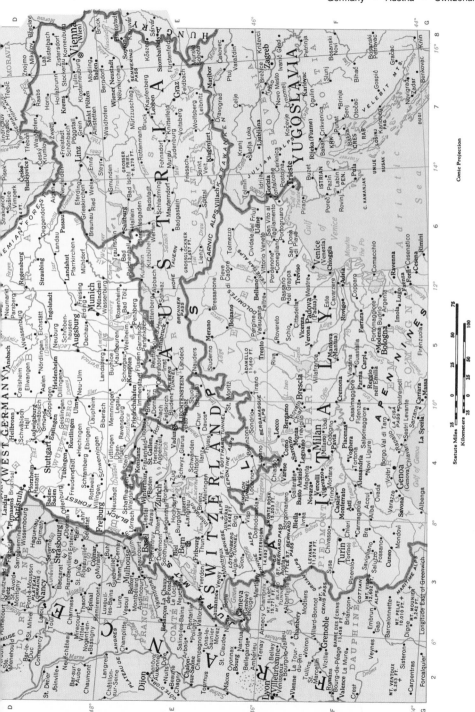

Conic Projection

Statute Miles

Kilometers

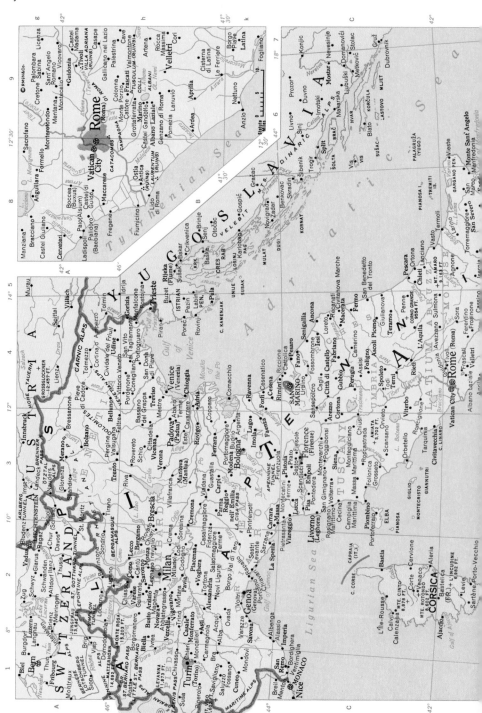

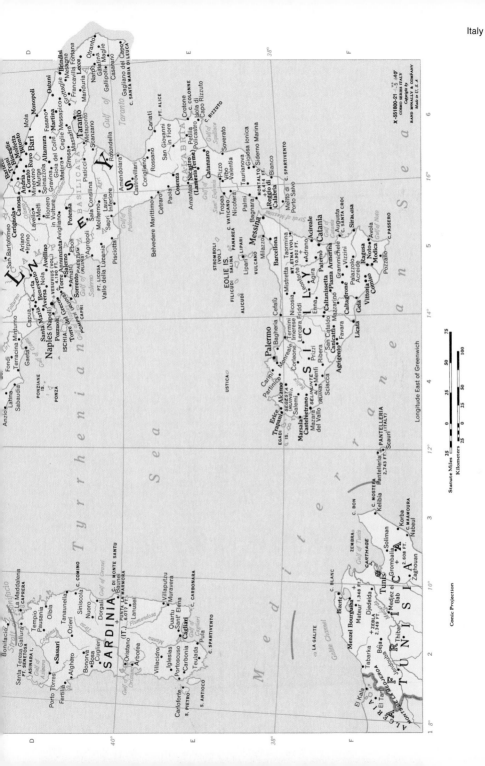

Conic Projection

Statute Miles 25 0 25 50 75

Kilometers 25 0 25 50 100

Longitude East of Greenwich

COSMO SERIES POLAND, CZECH.
Copyright by
RAND M⊂NALLY & COMPANY
Made in U. S. A.
X-559391-21 |7-|-11|

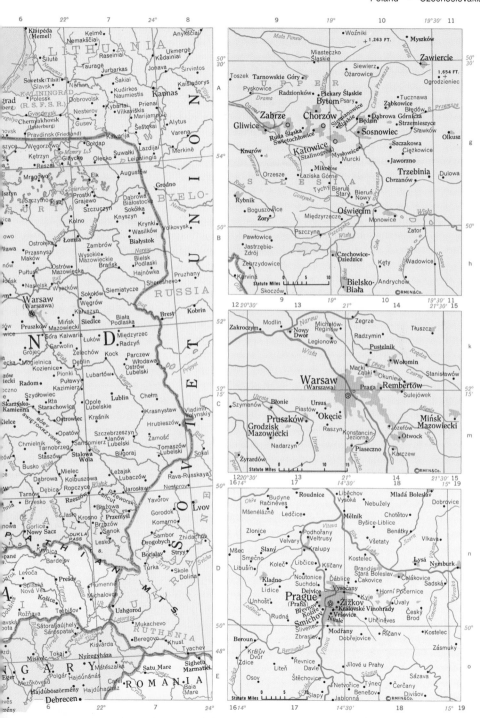

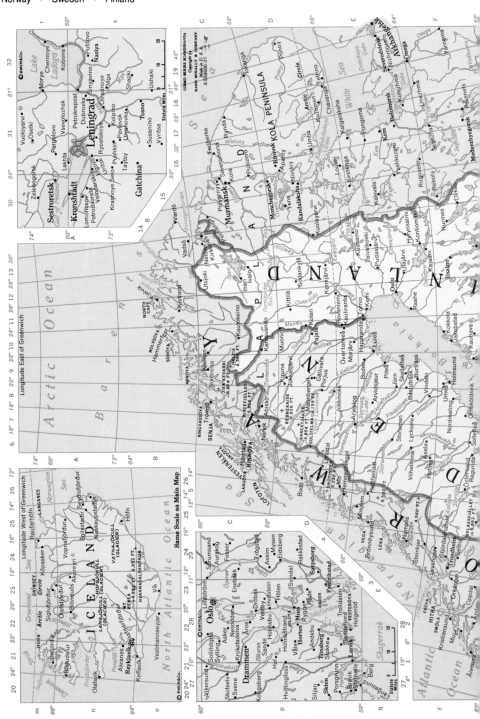

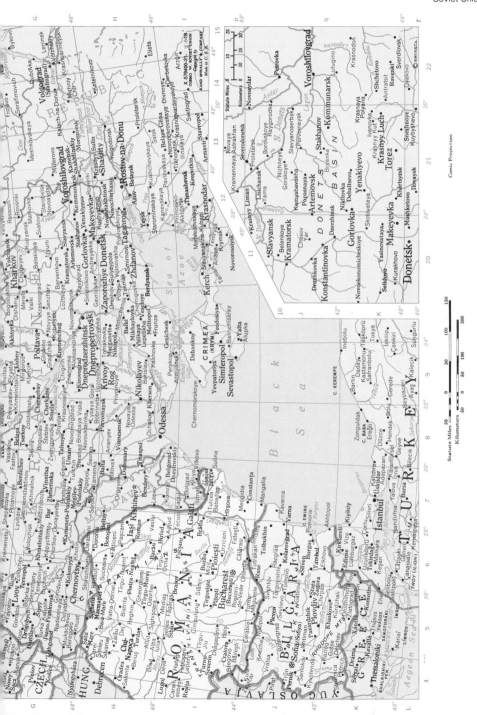

Conic Projection

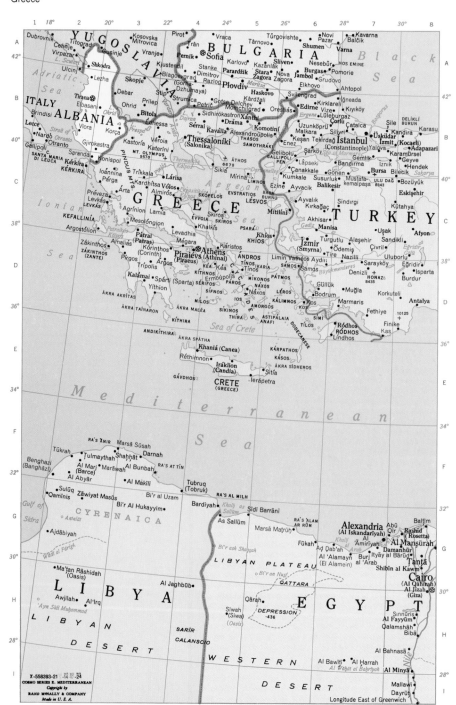

X-558393-21

COSMO SERIES E. MEDITERRANEAN
Copyright by
RAND McNALLY & COMPANY
Made in U.S.A.

Longitude East of Greenwich

GAZETTEER OF EUROPE

Ethnic groups, religions, trade partners, exports, and imports are listed in order of decreasing size and/or importance. Languages are similarly organized, with official language(s) listed first. Political parties are cited alphabetically, as are membership entries, which represent member nations of the following organizations:

Commonwealth of Nations (CW)
Council for Mutual Economic Assistance (CEMA)
North Atlantic Treaty Organization (NATO)
Organization for Economic Cooperation and Development (OECD)
United Nations (UN)

ALBANIA

Official name People's Socialist Republic of Albania

PEOPLE
Population 2,935,000. **Density** 264/mi² (102/km²). **Urban** 33%. **Capital** Tirana, 198,000. **Ethnic groups** Albanian 96%. **Languages** Albanian, Greek. **Religions** Muslim 70%, Albanian Orthodox 20%, Roman Catholic 10%. **Life expectancy** 72 female, 68 male. **Literacy** 75%.

POLITICS
Government Socialist republic. **Parties** Workers'. **Suffrage** Universal, over 18. **Memberships** UN. **Subdivisions** 26 districts.

ECONOMY
GNP $2,150,000,000. **Per capita** $820. **Monetary unit** Lek. **Trade partners** Yugoslavia, Czechoslovakia, Italy. **Exports** Asphalt, bitumen, petroleum products. **Imports** Machinery, machine tools, iron and steel products.

LAND
Description Southeastern Europe. **Area** 11,100 mi² (28,748 km²). **Highest point** Korab 9,026 ft (2,751 m). **Lowest point** Sea level.

People. A homogeneous native population characterizes Albania, with Greeks the main minority. Five centuries of Turkish rule shaped much of the culture and led many Albanians to adopt Islam. Since 1944, when the current Communist regime was established, an increased emphasis on education has more than tripled the literacy rate. In 1967 religious institutions were banned, and Albania claims to be the world's first atheist state.

Economy and the Land. Reputedly one of the poorest countries in Europe, Albania has tried to shift its economy from agriculture to industry. Farms employed about 60 percent of the work force in 1970, a significant decrease from more than 80 percent before 1944. Mineral resources make mining the chief industrial activity. The terrain consists of forested hills and mountains, and the climate is mild.

History and Politics. Early invaders and rulers included Greeks, Romans, Goths, and others. In 1468 the Ottoman Turks conquered the area, and it remained part of their empire until the First Balkan War in 1912. Invaded by Italy and occupied by Germany during World War II, Albania set up a Communist government in 1944, following the German retreat. A strict approach to communism caused the country to sever ties with its onetime allies—Yugoslavia, the Soviet Union, and most recently China—and today the country remains unallied. Relations with some nations have improved. ∎

ANDORRA

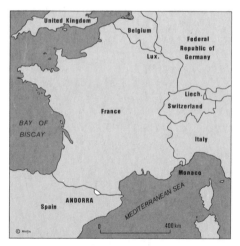

Official name Principality of Andorra

PEOPLE
Population 39,000. **Density** 223/mi² (86/km²). **Capital** Andorra, 14,928. **Ethnic groups** Spanish 61%, Andorran 30%, French 6%. **Languages** Catalan, Spanish, French. **Religions** Roman Catholic. **Literacy** 100%.

POLITICS
Government Coprincipality (France, Spain). **Parties** None. **Suffrage** Third-generation Andorrans, over 21. **Memberships** None. **Subdivisions** 7 districts.

ECONOMY

Monetary unit Spanish peseta, French franc. **Trade partners** Spain, France.

LAND

Description Southwestern Europe, landlocked. **Area** 175 mi^2 (453 km^2). **Highest point** Coma Pedrosa Pk, 9,665 ft (2,946 m). **Lowest point** Valira River valley, 2,756 ft (840 m).

People. Much of Andorran life and culture has been shaped by its mountainous terrain and governing countries, France and Spain. Population is concentrated in the valleys, and despite a tourism boom in the past decades, the peaks and valleys of the Pyrenees have isolated the small country from many twentieth-century changes. Catalan is the official language, and cultural and historic ties exist with the Catalonian region of northern Spain. The majority of the population is Spanish; Andorran citizens are a minority.

Economy and the Land. The terrain has established Andorra's economy as well as its life-style. Improved transportation routes together with other factors have resulted in a thriving tourist industry— a dramatic shift from traditional sheepherding and tobacco growing. In addition, duty-free status has made the country a European shopping mecca. Tobacco is still the main agricultural product, though only about 4 percent of the land is arable. Climate varies with altitude; winters are cold, and summers cool and pleasant.

History and Politics. Tradition indicates that Charlemagne freed the area from the Moors in A.D. 806. A French count and the Spanish bishop of Seo de Urgel signed an agreement in the 1200s to act as coprinces of the country, establishing the political status and boundaries that exist today. The coprincipality is governed by the president of France and the bishop of Seo de Urgel. The country has no formal constitution, no armed forces other than a small police force, and no political parties. ∎

AUSTRIA

Official name Republic of Austria

PEOPLE

Population 7,580,000. **Density** 234/mi^2 (90/km^2). **Urban** 55%. **Capital** Vienna, 1,515,666. **Ethnic groups** German 98%. **Languages** German. **Religions** Roman Catholic 85%, Protestant 7%. **Life expectancy** 76 female, 71 male. **Literacy** 98%.

POLITICS

Government Republic. **Parties** Communist, Liberal, People's, Socialist. **Suffrage** Universal, over 19. **Memberships** OECD, UN. **Subdivisions** 9 states.

ECONOMY

GNP $66,890,000,000. **Per capita** $10,995. **Monetary unit** Schilling. **Trade partners** West Germany, Italy, Eastern European countries. **Exports** Iron and steel products, machinery, wood. **Imports** Machinery, chemicals, textiles, clothing.

LAND

Description Central Europe, landlocked. **Area** 32,377 mi^2 (83,855 km^2). **Highest point** Grossglockner, 12,457 ft (3,797 m). **Lowest point** Neusiedler See, 377 ft (115 m).

People. Nearly all Austrians are native born, German speaking, and most are Roman Catholic, a homogeneity belying a history of invasions by diverse peoples. With a long cultural tradition, the country has contributed greatly to music and the arts; and Vienna, the capital, is one of the great cultural centers of Europe.

Economy and the Land. Austria's economy is a blend of state and privately owned industry. After World War II the government began nationalizing industries, returning many to the private sector as the economy stabilized. Unemployment is low, and the economy remains relatively strong. The economic mainstays are services and manufacturing. Agriculture is limited because of the overall mountainous terrain, with the Danube River basin in the east containing the most productive soils. The alpine landscape also attracts many tourists, as does the country's cultural heritage. The climate is generally moderate.

History and Politics. Early in its history, Austria was settled by Celts, ruled by Romans, and invaded by Germans, Slavs, Magyars, and others. Long rule by the Hapsburg family began in the thirteenth century, and in time Austria became the center of a vast empire. In 1867 Hungarian pressure resulted in the formation of the dual monarchy of Austria-Hungary. Nationalist movements against Austria culminated in the 1914 assassination of the heir to the throne, Archduke Francis Ferdinand, and set off the conflict that became World War I. In 1918 the war ended, the Hapsburg emperor was overthrown, Austria became a republic, and present-day boundaries were established. Political unrest and instability followed. In 1938 Adolf Hitler incorporated Austria into the German Reich. A period of occupation after World War II was followed by Austria's declaration of neutrality and ongoing political stability. Austria today frequently serves as a bridge for exchanges between Communist and non-Communist countries. ∎

BELGIUM

Official name Kingdom of Belgium
PEOPLE
Population 9,875,000. **Density** 838/mi² (324/km²).
Urban 95%. **Capital** Brussels, 137,738. **Ethnic groups** Fleming 55%, Walloon 33%, mixed and others 12%.

Languages Dutch (Flemish), French, German.
Religions Roman Catholic 75%. **Life expectancy** 75 female, 69 male. **Literacy** 98%.
POLITICS
Government Constitutional monarchy. **Parties** Flemish: Liberal, Social Christian, Socialist. Walloon: Liberal, Socialist. **Suffrage** Universal, over 18. **Memberships** NATO, OECD, UN. **Subdivisions** 9 provinces.
ECONOMY
GNP $85,420,000,000. **Per capita** $8,628. **Monetary unit** Franc. **Trade partners** West Germany, France, Netherlands. **Exports** Machinery, chemicals, food, livestock. **Imports** Machinery, fuels, food, motor vehicles.
LAND
Description Western Europe. **Area** 11,783 mi² (30,518 km²). **Highest point** Botrange, 2,277 ft (694 m). **Lowest point** Sea level.

People. Language separates Belgium into two main regions. Northern Belgium, known as Flanders, is dominated by Flemings, Flemish-speaking descendants of Germanic Franks. French-speaking Walloons, descendants of the Celts, inhabit southern Belgium, or Wallonia. Both groups are found in centrally located Brussels. In addition, a small German-speaking population is concentrated in the east. Flemish and French divisions often result in discord, but diversity has also been a source of cultural richness. Belgium has often been at the hub of European cultural movements.

Economy and the Land. The economy as well as the population was affected by Belgium's location at the center of European activity. Industry was early established as the economic base, and today the country is heavily industrialized. Although agriculture plays a minor economic role, Belgium is nearly self-sufficient in food production. The north and west are dominated by a flat fertile plain, the central region by rolling hills, and the south by the Ardennes Forest, often a tourist destination. The climate is cool and temperate.

History and Politics. Belgium's history began with the settlement of the Belgae tribe in the second century B.C. The Romans invaded the area around 50 B.C. and were overthrown by Germanic Franks in the A.D. 400s. Trade, manufacturing, and art prospered as various peoples invaded, passed through, and ruled the area. In 1794 Napoleon annexed Belgium to France. He was defeated at Waterloo in Belgium in 1815, and the country passed into Dutch hands. Dissatisfaction under Netherland rule led to revolt and, in 1830, the formation of the independent country of Belgium. The country was overrun by Germans during both world wars. Linguistic divisions mark nearly all political activity, from parties split by language to government decisions based on linguistic rivalries. ∎

BULGARIA

Official name People's Republic of Bulgaria
PEOPLE
Population 8,980,000. **Density** 210/mi² (81/km²). **Urban** 64%. **Capital** Sofia, 1,056,945. **Ethnic groups** Bulgarian 85%, Turkish 9%, Gypsy 3%, Macedonian 3%. **Languages** Bulgarian. **Religions** Bulgarian Orthodox 85%, Muslim 13%. **Life expectancy** 75 female, 71 male. **Literacy** 95%.
POLITICS
Government Socialist republic. **Parties** Communist. **Suffrage** Universal, over 18. **Memberships** CEMA, UN, Warsaw Pact. **Subdivisions** 27 provinces, 1 city.
ECONOMY
GNP $35,300,000,000. **Per capita** $3,963. **Monetary unit** Lev. **Trade partners** U.S.S.R., Eastern European countries, West Germany. **Exports** Machinery, agricultural products, fuels. **Imports** Fuels, machinery, transportation equipment.
LAND
Description Southeastern Europe. **Area** 42,823 mi² (110,912 km²). **Highest point** Musala, 9,596 ft (2,925 m). **Lowest point** Sea level.

People. Bulgaria's ethnic composition was determined early in its history when Bulgar tribes conquered the area's Slavic inhabitants. Bulgarians, descendants of these peoples, are a majority today, and Turks, Gypsies, and Macedonians compose the main minority groups. Postwar development is reflected in an agriculture-to-industry shift in employment and a resultant rural-to-urban population movement.

Economy and the Land. Following World War II, the Bulgarian government began a program of expansion, turning the undeveloped agricultural nation into an industrial state modeled after the Soviet Union. Today the industrial sector is the greatest economic contributor and employer. Farming, however, continues to play an economic role. A climate similar to that of the American Midwest and rich soils in river valleys are suited for raising livestock and growing grain and other crops. The overall terrain is mountainous.

History and Politics. The area of modern Bulgaria had been absorbed by the Roman Empire by A.D. 15 and was subsequently invaded by the Slavs. In the seventh century Bulgars conquered the region and settled alongside Slavic inhabitants. Rule by the Ottoman Turks began in the late fourteenth century and lasted until 1878, when the Bulgarians defeated the Turks with the aid of Russia and Romania. The Principality of Bulgaria emerged in 1885, with boundaries approximating those of today, and in 1908 Bulgaria was declared an independent kingdom. A desire for access to the Aegean Sea and increased territory was partially responsible for Bulgaria's involvement in the Balkan Wars of 1912 and 1913 and alliances with Germany during both world wars. Following Bulgaria's declaration of war on the United States and Britain in World War II, the Soviet Union declared war on Bulgaria. Defeat came in 1944, the monarchy was overthrown, and a Communist government established shortly thereafter. Foreign policy is guided by alliance with the Soviet Union and other Communist nations, but lately more attention has been given to relations with Western European countries and developing nations in Africa and the Middle East. ∎

CZECHOSLOVAKIA

Official name Czechoslovak Socialist Republic
PEOPLE
Population 15,490,000. **Density** 314/mi² (121/km²). **Urban** 67%. **Capital** Prague, 1,185,693. **Ethnic groups** Czech 65%, Slovak 30%, Hungarian 3%. **Languages** Czech, Slovak, Hungarian. **Religions** Roman Catholic 77%, Protestant 20%, Greek Orthodox 2%. **Life expectancy** 74 female, 67 male. **Literacy** 99%.
POLITICS
Government Socialist republic. **Parties** Communist. **Suffrage** Universal, over 18. **Memberships** CEMA, UN, Warsaw Pact. **Subdivisions** 2 semiautonomous republics.
ECONOMY
GNP $147,100,000,000. **Per capita** $9,550. **Monetary unit** Koruna. **Trade partners** U.S.S.R., East Germany,

Poland, Hungary, West Germany. **Exports** Machinery, transportation equipment, iron and steel, consumer goods. **Imports** Fuels, machinery, raw materials, transportation equipment.

LAND

Description Eastern Europe, landlocked. **Area** 49,381 mi² (127,896 km²). **Highest point** Gerlachovka, 8,711 ft (2,655 m). **Lowest point** Bodrog River, 308 ft (94 m).

People. Czechs and Slovaks, descendants of Slavic tribes, predominate in Czechoslovakia. Characterized by a German-influenced culture, Czechs are concentrated in the regions of Bohemia and Moravia. Slovaks, whose culture was influenced by Hungarian Magyars, reside mainly in Slovakia. Both Czech and Slovak are official languages. Minorities include Hungarians, or Magyars; Ukrainians; Germans; Poles; and Gypsies, a rapidly growing group concentrated in Slovakia. Most people are Roman Catholic, and the government licenses and pays clergy.

Economy and the Land. An industrial nation, Czechoslovakia has a centralized economy and one of the highest standards of living among Communist countries. Coal deposits in Bohemia and Moravia provided a base for industrial development, and Bohemia remains an economically important region. Nearly all agriculture is collectivized, and farm output includes grains, potatoes, sugar beets, and livestock. Farming areas are found in the river valleys of north-central Bohemia and central Moravia, and Slovakia remains largely agricultural. Czechoslovakia's terrain is characterized by a rolling western area, low mountains in the north and south, central hills, and the Carpathian Mountains in the east. The climate is temperate.

History and Politics. Slavic tribes were established in the region by the sixth century. By the tenth century Hungarian Magyars had conquered the Slovaks in the region of Slovakia. Bohemia and Moravia became part of the Holy Roman Empire, and by the twelfth century Bohemia had become a strong kingdom that included Moravia and parts of Austria and Poland. Austria gained control of the area in 1620, and it later became part of Austria-Hungary. With the collapse of Austria-Hungary at the end of World War I, an independent Czechoslovakia consisting of Bohemia, Moravia, and Slovakia was formed. Nazi Germany invaded Czechoslovakia in 1939, and the Soviet Union liberated the nation from German occupation in the winter and spring of 1944 to 1945. By 1948 Communists controlled the government, and political purges continued from 1949 to 1952. A 1968 invasion by the Soviet Union and Bulgaria, Hungary, Poland, and East Germany resulted when the Czechoslovakian Communist party leader introduced liberal reforms. Efforts to eliminate dissent continued into the seventies. Foreign policy closely follows that of the Soviet Union.   ■

DENMARK

Official name Kingdom of Denmark
PEOPLE
Population 5,010,000. **Density** 301/mi² (116/km²). **Urban** 83%. **Capital** Copenhagen, 498,850. **Ethnic**

groups Scandinavian. **Languages** Danish. **Religions** Lutheran 97%. **Life expectancy** 77 female, 73 male. **Literacy** 99%.

POLITICS
Government Constitutional monarchy. **Parties** Conservative, Liberal, Social Democratic, Socialist People's. **Suffrage** Universal, over 21. **Memberships** NATO, OECD, UN. **Subdivisions** 14 counties, 2 cities.

ECONOMY
GNP $56,400,000,000. **Per capita** $11,016. **Monetary unit** Krone. **Trade partners** West Germany, U.K., Sweden, U.S., Norway. **Exports** Meat and dairy products, machinery, transportation equipment, textiles. **Imports** Raw materials, fuels, machinery, transportation equipment.

LAND
Description Northern Europe. **Area** 16,633 mi² (43,080 km²). **Highest point** Yding Skovhøj, 568 ft (173 m). **Lowest point** Lammefjord, 23 ft (7 m) below sea level. *The above information excludes the Faeroe Islands.*

People. Denmark is made up of the Jutland Peninsula and more than four hundred islands, about one hundred of which are inhabited. In addition to nearby islands, Greenland, situated northeast of Canada, and the Faeroe Islands, between Scotland and Iceland in the North Atlantic, are part of Denmark. Lutheran, Danish-speaking Scandinavians constitute the homogeneous population of the peninsula and surrounding islands, although a German minority is concentrated near the West German border. Faeroese-speaking people inhabit the Faeroe Islands. The literacy rate is high, and Denmark has made significant contributions to science, literature, and the arts.

Economy and the Land. Despite limited natural resources, Denmark has a diversified economy. Agriculture contributes to trade, and pork and bacon are important products. Postwar expansion focused on industry, and the country now imports the raw materials it lacks and exports finished products. The North Sea is the site of oil and natural-gas deposits. On the Faeroe Islands, traditional fishing continues as the economic mainstay. Most of Denmark's terrain is rolling, with hills covering much of the peninsula and the nearby islands. Coastal regions are marked by fjords and sandy beaches, especially in the west. The climate is temperate, with North Sea winds moderating temperatures. The rugged Faeroe Islands are damp, cloudy, and windy.

History and Politics. By the first century access to the sea had brought contact with other civilizations and led to the Viking era, lasting from the ninth to eleventh centuries and resulting in temporary Danish rule of England. In the fourteenth century, Sweden, Norway, Finland, Iceland, the Faeroe Islands, and Greenland were united under Danish rule. Sweden and Finland withdrew from the union in the 1500s, and Denmark lost Norway to Sweden in 1814. A constitutional monarchy was instituted in 1849. Late nineteenth-century social reform, reflected in a new constitution in 1915, laid the groundwork for Denmark's current welfare state. The country remained neutral during World War I. Iceland gained independence following the war but maintained its union with Denmark until 1944. Despite declared neutrality during World War II, Denmark was invaded by Germany in 1940 and occupied until 1945. Compromise and gradual change characterize Danish politics, and foreign policy emphasizes relations with developing nations and peaceful solutions to international problems. ∎

FINLAND

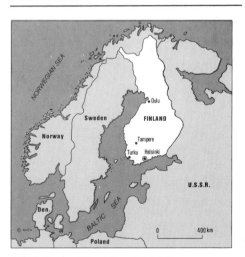

Official name Republic of Finland

PEOPLE
Population 4,885,000. **Density** 37/mi² (14/km²). **Urban** 60%. **Capital** Helsinki, 483,051. **Ethnic groups** Finnish, Swedish, Lappish. **Languages** Finnish, Swedish. **Religions** Lutheran 97%, Greek Orthodox 1%. **Life expectancy** 78 female, 69 male. **Literacy** 100%.

POLITICS
Government Republic. **Parties** Center, National Coalition, People's Democratic League, Social Democratic. **Suffrage** Universal, over 18. **Memberships** OECD, UN. **Subdivisions** 12 provinces.

ECONOMY
GNP $49,100,000,000. **Per capita** $10,124. **Monetary unit** Markka. **Trade partners** U.S.S.R., Sweden, West Germany, U.K. **Exports** Wood, paper and wood pulp, machinery. **Imports** Fuels, chemicals, machinery, food.

LAND
Description Northern Europe. **Area** 130,558 mi² (338,145 km²). **Highest point** Haltia, 4,357 ft (1,328 m). **Lowest point** Sea level.

People. As a result of past Swedish rule, the mainly Finnish population includes minorities of Swedes, in addition to indigenous Lapps. Because part of northern Finland lies in the Arctic Circle, population is concentrated in the south. Finland's rich cultural tradition has contributed much to the arts, and its highly developed social-welfare programs provide free education through the university level and nationalized health insurance.

Economy and the Land. Much of Finland's economy is based on its rich forests, which support trade and manufacturing activities. The steel industry is also important. Agriculture focuses on dairy farming and livestock raising; hence many fruits and vegetables must be imported. Coastal islands and lowlands, a central lake region, and northern hills mark Finland's scenic terrain. Summers in the south and central regions are warm, and winters long and cold. Northern Finland—located in the Land of the Midnight Sun—has periods of uninterrupted daylight in summer and darkness in winter.

History and Politics. The indigenous nomadic Lapps migrated north in the first century when the Finns arrived, probably from west-central Russia. A Russian-Swedish struggle for control of the area ended with Swedish rule in the 1100s. Finland was united with Denmark from the fourteenth through the sixteenth centuries, and from the sixteenth through the eighteenth centuries Russia and Sweden fought several wars for control of the country. In 1809 Finland became an autonomous grand duchy within the Russian Empire. The Russian czar was overthrown in the 1917 Bolshevik Revolution, and Finland's declaration of independence was recognized by the new Russian government. During World War II Finland fought against the Soviets and, by the peace treaty signed in 1947, lost a portion of its land to the Soviet Union. During the postwar years Finland and Russia renewed their economic and cultural ties and signed an agreement of friendship and cooperation. Foreign policy emphasizes friendly relations with the U.S.S.R. and Scandinavia. ∎

FRANCE

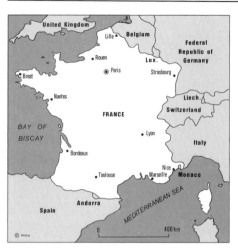

Official name French Republic

PEOPLE
Population 55,020,000. **Density** 261/mi² (101/km²). **Urban** 73%. **Capital** Paris, 2,176,243. **Ethnic groups** Celtic, Latin. **Languages** French. **Religions** Roman Catholic 90%, Protestant 2%. **Life expectancy** 78 female, 70 male. **Literacy** 99%.

POLITICS
Government Republic. **Parties** Communist, Rally for the Republic, Socialist, Union for Democracy. **Suffrage** Universal, over 18. **Memberships** NATO, OECD, UN. **Subdivisions** 96 departments.

ECONOMY
GDP $542,000,000,000. **Per capita** $9,996. **Monetary unit** Franc. **Trade partners** West Germany, Italy, Belgium, Luxembourg, U.S., U.K. **Exports** Machinery, transportation equipment, food. **Imports** Petroleum, machinery, chemicals.

LAND
Description Western Europe. **Area** 211,208 mi² (547,026 km²). **Highest point** Mt. Blanc, 15,771 ft (4,807 m). **Lowest point** Étang de Cazaux, 10 ft (3 m) below sea level.

The above information excludes French overseas departments.

People. Many centuries ago Celtic tribes, Germanic tribes, and Latins established France's current ethnic patterns. The French language developed from the Latin of invading Romans but includes Celtic and Germanic influences as well. Language and customs vary somewhat from region to region, but most people who speak dialects also speak French. France has long contributed to learning and the arts, and Paris is a world cultural center. In addition to mainland divisions, the country has overseas departments and territories.

Economy and the Land. The French economy is highly developed. The nation is a leader in agriculture and industry, and its problems of inflation and unemployment are common to other modern countries. Soils in the north and northeast are especially productive, and grapes are grown in the south. Minerals include iron ore and bauxite. Industry is diversified, centered in the Paris manufacturing area, and tourism is also important. About two-thirds of the country is flat to rolling, and about one-third is mountainous, including the Pyrenees in the south and the Alps in the east. In the west and north winters are cool and summers mild. Climate varies with altitude in the mountains. The southern coast has a Mediterranean climate with hot summers and mild winters.

History and Politics. In ancient times Celtic tribes inhabited the area that encompasses present-day France. The Romans, who called the region Gaul, began to invade about 200 B.C., and by the 50s B.C. the entire region had come under Roman rule. Northern Germanic tribes—including the Franks, Visigoths, and Burgundians—spread throughout the region as Roman control weakened, and the Franks defeated the Romans in A.D. 486. In the 800s Charlemagne greatly expanded Frankish-controlled territory, which was subsequently divided into three kingdoms. The western kingdom and part of the central kingdom included modern France. In 987 the Capetian dynasty began when Hugh Capet came to the throne, an event which is often considered the start of the French nation. During subsequent centuries the power of the kings increased, and France became a leading world power. Ambitious projects, such as the palace built by Louis XIV at Versailles, and several military campaigns resulted in financial difficulties. The failing economy and divisions between rich and poor led to the French Revolution in 1789 and the First French Republic in 1792. Napoleon Bonaparte, who had gained prominence during the revolution, overthrew the government in 1799 and established the First Empire, which ended in 1815 with his defeat at Waterloo in Belgium. The subsequent monarchy resulted in discontent, and a 1848 revolution established the Second French Republic with an elected president, who in turn proclaimed himself emperor and set up the Second Empire in 1852. Following a war with Prussia in 1870, the emperor was ousted, and the Third Republic began. This republic endured Germany's invasion in World War I but ended in 1940 when invading Germans defeated the French. By 1942 the Nazis had control of the entire country. The Allies liberated France in 1944, and General Charles de Gaulle

headed a provisional government until 1946, when the Fourth Republic was established. Colonial revolts in Africa and French Indochina took their toll on the economy during the fifties, and controversy over a continuing Algerian war for independence brought de Gaulle to power once more and resulted in the Fifth Republic in 1958. Dissension and national strikes erupted during the 1960s, a result of dissatisfaction with the government, and de Gaulle resigned in 1969. In 1981 the country elected a Socialist president. France is active in European foreign relations and continues to play a role in its former African colonies. ∎

GERMANY, EAST

Official name German Democratic Republic
PEOPLE
Population 16,600,000. **Density** 397/mi² (153/km²).
Urban 76%. **Capital** East Berlin, 1,152,529. **Ethnic groups** German. **Languages** German. **Religions** Protestant 47%, Roman Catholic 7%. **Life expectancy** 75 female, 69 male. **Literacy** 99%.
POLITICS
Government Socialist republic. **Parties** Socialist Unity. **Suffrage** Universal, over 18. **Memberships** CEMA, UN, Warsaw Pact. **Subdivisions** 14 districts, 1 independent city.
ECONOMY
GNP $165,600,000,000. **Per capita** $9,903. **Monetary unit** Mark. **Trade partners** U.S.S.R., Eastern European

countries, West Germany. **Exports** Machinery, chemical products, textiles. **Imports** Raw materials, machinery, fuels.

LAND
Description Eastern Europe. **Area** 41,768 mi² (108,179 km²). **Highest point** Fichtelberg, 3,983 ft (1,214 m). **Lowest point** Sea level.

People. The population of East Germany is mainly German and German speaking. A small minority of Slavs exists. East Germans are mostly Protestant, especially Lutheran, although many people remain religiously unaffiliated. The standard of living is relatively high, and citizens benefit from extensive educational and social-insurance systems. The arts also receive much government and public support. The people of East and West Germany are divided by a guarded border but share a cultural heritage of achievements in music, literature, philosophy, and science.

Economy and the Land. Postwar economic expansion emphasized industry, and today East Germany is one of the world's largest industrial producers. The economy is centralized: industry is state owned and most agriculture is collectivized. Mineral resources are limited. The terrain is marked by northern lakes and low hills; central mountains, productive plains, and sandy stretches; and southern uplands. The climate is temperate.

History and Politics. History of East and West Germany follows WEST GERMANY.

GERMANY, WEST

Official name Federal Republic of Germany
PEOPLE
Population 61,390,000. **Density** 639/mi² (247/km²). **Urban** 94%. **Capital** Bonn, 293,852. **Ethnic groups** German. **Languages** German. **Religions** Roman Catholic 45%, Protestant 44%. **Life expectancy** 76 female, 70 male. **Literacy** 99%.

POLITICS
Government Republic. **Parties** Christian Democratic Union, Christian Social Union, Free Democratic, Social Democratic. **Suffrage** Universal, over 18. **Memberships** NATO, OECD, UN. **Subdivisions** 11 states.

ECONOMY
GNP $658,400,000,000. **Per capita** $10,682. **Monetary unit** Deutsche mark. **Trade partners** Western European countries, U.S. **Exports** Machinery, motor vehicles, chemicals, iron and steel products. **Imports** Manufactured goods, fuels, raw materials.

LAND
Description Western Europe. **Area** 96,019 mi² (248,687 km²). **Highest point** Zugspitze, 9,721 ft (2,963 m).

Lowest point Freepsum Lake, 7 ft (2 m) below sea level.

People. West Germany, like East Germany, is homogeneous, with a Germanic, German-speaking population. Religious groups include Roman Catholics and mostly Lutheran Protestants. The populace is generally well educated. The country is about twice as large as East Germany and has about four times the population.

Economy and the Land. Despite destruction incurred in World War II and Germany's division into

two countries, West Germany has one of the world's strongest economies. Industry provides the basis for prosperity, with mining, manufacturing, construction, and utilities important contributors. The Ruhr district is the nation's most important industrial region, situated near the Ruhr River in northwest-central Germany and including cities such as Essen and Dortmund. The Rhine River, the most important commercial waterway in Europe, is found in the west. Agriculture remains important in the south. Germany's terrain varies from northern plains to western and central uplands and hills that extend to the southern Bavarian Alps. The dark green firs of the Black Forest lie in the southwest. The mild climate is tempered by the sea in the north, and in the south the winters are colder because of proximity to the Alps.

History and Politics. In ancient times Germanic tribes overcame Celtic inhabitants in the area of Germany and established a northern stronghold against Roman expansion of Gaul. As the Roman Empire weakened, the Germanic peoples invaded, deposing the Roman governor of Gaul in the fifth century A.D. The Franks composed the strongest tribe, and in the ninth century Frankish-controlled territory was expanded and united under Charlemagne. The 843 Treaty of Verdun divided Charlemagne's lands into three kingdoms, with the eastern territory encompassing modern Germany. Unity did not follow, however, and Germany remained a disjointed territory of feudal states, duchies, and independent cities. The Reformation, a movement led by German monk Martin Luther, began in 1517 and evolved into the Protestant branch of Christianity. In the eighteenth century the state of Prussia became the foremost rival of the powerful Austrian state. The rise of Prussian power and growing nationalism eventually united the German states into the German Empire in 1871, and Prussian chancellor Otto von Bismarck installed Prussian king Wilhelm I as emperor. Reconciliation with Austria-Hungary came in 1879, and Germany allied with Austria in World War I in 1914. The empire collapsed as a result of the war, and the Weimar Republic was established in 1919. Instability and disunity arose in the face of economic problems. Promising prosperity and encouraging nationalism, Adolf Hitler of the National Socialist, or Nazi, party became chancellor in 1933. Hitler did away with the freedoms of speech and assembly and began a genocidal program to eliminate Jews and other peoples. Hitler's ambitions led to World War II; and in April 1945 Hitler committed suicide, and in May Germany unconditionally surrendered to the Allies. The United States, Britain, the Soviet Union, and France divided Germany into four zones of occupation.

East Germany. After World War II, eastern Germany was designated the Soviet-occupied zone. The Communist party combined with the Social Democrats and, following the formation of the western Federal Republic of Germany in 1949, the eastern region proclaimed itself the German Democratic Republic. In 1955 the country became fully independent. Berlin, not included in the occupation zones, was a separate entity under the four Allied nations. When the Soviet Union ceased to participate in Allied negotiations in 1948, the city was divided. The Berlin Wall, constructed in 1961, separates East from West Berlin.

West Germany. The Federal Republic of Germany was established in 1949, composed of the American-, French-, and British-occupied zones. The republic became fully independent in 1955. Military forces of the United States, France, and Britain continue to occupy West Berlin. West German politics have been marked by stability under various chancellors. The Green party, formed in the 1970s by environmentalists, has grown in importance in the 1980s. ∎

GREECE

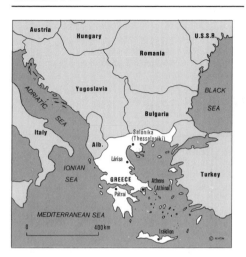

Official name Hellenic Republic
PEOPLE
Population 10,030,000. **Density** 197/mi² (76/km²). **Urban** 65%. **Capital** Athens, 885,737. **Ethnic groups** Greek 98%, Turkish 1%. **Languages** Greek. **Religions** Greek Orthodox 98%, Muslim 1%. **Life expectancy** 76 female, 72 male. **Literacy** 95%.
POLITICS
Government Republic. **Parties** Communist, New Democracy, Panhellenic Socialist Movement. **Suffrage** Universal, over 18. **Memberships** NATO, OECD, UN. **Subdivisions** 51 departments.
ECONOMY
GNP $38,600,000,000. **Per capita** $3,959. **Monetary unit** Drachma. **Trade partners** West Germany, Italy, France, U.S. **Exports** Textiles, fruits, minerals. **Imports** Machinery, transportation equipment, petroleum, chemicals, consumer goods.
LAND
Description Southeastern Europe. **Area** 50,944 mi² (131,944 km²). **Highest point** Mt. Olympus, 9,570 ft (2,917 m). **Lowest point** Sea level.

People. Greece has played a central role in European, African, and Asian cultures for thousands of years, but today its population is almost homogeneous. Native Greek inhabitants are united by a language that dates back three thousand years and a religion that influences many aspects of everyday life. Athens, the capital, was the cultural center of an ancient civilization that produced masterpieces of art and literature and broke ground in philosophy, political thought, and science.

Economy and the Land. The economy of Greece takes its shape from terrain and location. Dominated by the sea and long a maritime trading power,

Greece has one of the largest merchant fleets in the world and depends greatly on commerce. The mountainous terrain and poor soil limit agriculture, although Greece is a leading producer of lemons and olives. The service sector, including tourism, provides most of Greece's national income. Inhabitants enjoy a temperate climate, with mild, wet winters, and hot, dry summers.

History and Politics. Greece's history begins with the early Bronze Age cultures of the Minoans and the Mycenaeans. The city-state, or polis, began to develop around the tenth century B.C., and Athens, a democracy, and Sparta, an oligarchy, gradually emerged as Greece's leaders. The Persian Wars, in which the city-states united to repel a vastly superior army, ushered in the Golden Age of Athens, a cultural explosion in the fifth century B.C. The Parthenon, perhaps Greece's most famous building, was built at this time. Athens was defeated by Sparta in the Peloponnesian War, and by 338 B.C. Philip II of Macedon had conquered all of Greece. His son, Alexander the Great, defeated the Persians and spread Greek civilization and language all over the known world. Greece became a Roman province in 146 B.C. and part of the Byzantine Empire in A.D. 395, but its traditions had a marked influence on these empires. Absorbed into the Ottoman Empire in the 1450s, Greece had gained independence by 1830 and became a constitutional monarchy about fifteen years later. For much of the twentieth century the nation was divided between republicans and monarchists. During World War II Germany occupied Greece, and postwar instability led to a civil war, with Communist rebels eventually losing. Greece was ruled by a repressive military junta from 1967 until 1974, when the regime relinquished power to a civilian government. The Greeks then voted for a republic over a monarchy. A Socialist government was elected in 1981. ■

HUNGARY

Official name Hungarian People's Republic
PEOPLE
Population 10,675,000. **Density** 297/mi² (115/km²).
Urban 54%. **Capital** Budapest, 2,064,000. **Ethnic groups** Hungarian 92%, Gypsy 3%, German 3%.
Languages Hungarian. **Religions** Roman Catholic 68%, Calvinist 20%, Lutheran 5%. **Life expectancy** 73 female, 66 male. **Literacy** 98%.
POLITICS
Government Socialist republic. **Parties** Socialist Workers'. **Suffrage** Universal, over 18. **Memberships** CEMA, UN, Warsaw Pact. **Subdivisions** 19 counties, 1 city.

ECONOMY
GNP $65,200,000,000. **Per capita** $6,901. **Monetary unit** Forint. **Trade partners** U.S.S.R., West Germany, East Germany. **Exports** Machinery, transportation equipment, agricultural products. **Imports** Machinery, transportation equipment, fuels, chemicals.
LAND
Description Eastern Europe, landlocked. **Area** 35,921 mi² (93,036 km²). **Highest point** Kékes, 3,330 ft (1,015 m). **Lowest point** Tisza River valley, 259 ft (79 m).

People. Hungary's major ethnic group and language evolved from Magyar tribes who settled the region in the ninth century. Gypsies, Germans, and other peoples compose minorities. Most people are Roman Catholic, and the government supervises religious activities through a state office. The government also controls educational programs, and the literacy rate is high. Growth of industry since the 1940s has caused a rural-to-urban population shift.

Economy and the Land. Following World War II, Hungary pursued a program of industrialization, and the onetime agricultural nation now looks to industry as its main economic contributor. Agriculture is almost completely socialized, and farming remains important, with productivity aided by fertile soils and a mild climate. Economic planning was decentralized in 1968, thus Hungary's economy differs from that of other Soviet-bloc nations. A flat plain dominates the landscape, and the lack of varying physical features results in a temperate climate throughout the country.

History and Politics. In the late 800s Magyar tribes from the east overcame Slavic and Germanic residents and settled the area. In the thirteenth century invading Mongols caused much destruction, and in the early 1500s, after repeated attacks, the Ottoman Turks gained domination of central Hungary. By the late seventeenth century the entire region had come under the rule of Austria's Hapsburgs. In 1867 Hungary succeeded in obtaining equal status with Austria, and the dual monarchy of Austria-Hungary emerged. Discontent and nationalistic demands increased until 1914, when a Bosnian Serb killed the heir to the Austro-Hungarian throne. Austria-Hungary declared war on Serbia, and World War I began, resulting in a loss of territory and population for Hungary. At the end of the war, in 1918, Hungary became a republic, only to revert to monarchical rule in 1919. Hungary entered World War II on the side of Germany, and Adolf Hitler set up a pro-Nazi government in Hungary in 1944. The Soviet Union invaded that same year, and a Hungarian-Allied peace treaty was signed in 1947. Coalition rule evolved into a Communist government in 1949. Discontent erupted into rebellion in 1956, a new premier declared Hungary neutral, and Soviet forces entered Budapest to quell the uprising. Since the early sixties, the standard of living has improved and economic and cultural liberties have increased. The country remains allied with the Soviet Union, and Western ties are expanding. ∎

ICELAND

Official name Republic of Iceland
PEOPLE
Population 240,000. **Density** 6/mi² (2.3/km²). **Urban** 89%. **Capital** Reykjavík, 84,593. **Ethnic groups** Mixed Norwegian and Celtic. **Languages** Icelandic. **Religions** Lutheran 95%. **Life expectancy** 80 female, 74 male. **Literacy** 100%.
POLITICS
Government Republic. **Parties** Independence, People's Alliance, Progressive, Social Democratic. **Suffrage** Universal, over 20. **Memberships** NATO, OECD, UN. **Subdivisions** 8 regions.
ECONOMY
GNP $2,200,000,000. **Per capita** $9,322. **Monetary unit** Króna. **Trade partners** U.S., Scandinavian countries, U.K., West Germany. **Exports** Fish and fish products, animal products, aluminum. **Imports** Machinery, transportation equipment, petroleum, food, textiles.
LAND
Description North Atlantic island. **Area** 39,769 mi² (103,000 km²). **Highest point** Hvannadalshnúkur, 6,952 ft (2,119 m). **Lowest point** Sea level.

People. Most Icelanders are of Norwegian or Celtic ancestry, live in coastal cities, and belong to the Lutheran church. Icelandic, the predominant language, has changed little from the Old Norse of the original settlers and still resembles the language of twelfth-century Nordic sagas.

Economy and the Land. Fish, found in the island's rich coastal waters, are the main natural resource and export. Iceland has a long tradition based on fishing, but the industry has recently suffered from decreasing markets and catches. Glaciers, lakes, hot springs, volcanoes, and a lava desert limit agricultural land but provide a scenic terrain. Although the island lies just south of the Arctic Circle, the climate is moderated by the Gulf Stream. Summers are damp and cool, and winters relatively mild but windy. Proximity to the Arctic Circle puts Iceland in the Land of the Midnight Sun, resulting in periods of twenty-four-hour daylight in June.

History and Politics. Norwegians began settlement of Iceland around the ninth century. The world's oldest parliament, the Althing, was established in Iceland in A.D. 930. Civil wars and instability during the thirteenth century led to the end of independence in 1262, when Iceland came under Norwegian rule. In the fourteenth century Norway was joined to Denmark's realm, and rule of Iceland passed to the Danes. The Althing was abolished in 1800 but re-established in 1843. In the 1918 Act of Union, Iceland became a sovereign state but retained its union with Denmark under a common king. Germany occupied Denmark in 1940, during World War II; and British troops, replaced by Americans in 1941, protected Iceland from invasion. Following a 1944 plebiscite, Iceland left its union with Denmark and became an independent republic. The country has no military. ∎

IRELAND

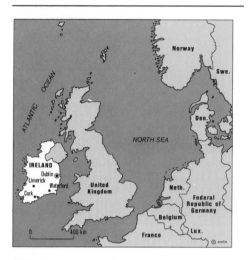

Official name Ireland
PEOPLE
Population 3,595,000. **Density** 132/mi² (51/km²). **Urban** 56%. **Capital** Dublin, 525,882. **Ethnic groups** Celtic, English. **Languages** Irish Gaelic, English. **Religions** Roman Catholic 94%, Anglican 4%. **Life expectancy** 75 female, 71 male. **Literacy** 99%.
POLITICS
Government Republic. **Parties** Fianna Fail, Fine Gael, Labor. **Suffrage** Universal, over 18. **Memberships** OECD, UN. **Subdivisions** 26 counties.
ECONOMY
GNP $17,000,000,000. **Per capita** $5,667. **Monetary unit** Pound. **Trade partners** U.K., other Western European countries, U.S. **Exports** Meat and dairy products, textiles, machinery. **Imports** Petroleum, petroleum products, machinery, chemicals, manufactured goods.
LAND
Description Northwestern Europe (five-sixths of island of Ireland). **Area** 27,136 mi² (70,283 km²). **Highest point** Carrauntoohil, 3,406 ft (1,038 m). **Lowest point** Sea level.

People. Most of Ireland's population is descended from the Celts, a people who flourished in Europe and Great Britain in ancient times. Irish Gaelic, a form of ancient Celtic, and English are official languages. Most people are Roman Catholic, and Protestants mainly belong to the Church of Ireland, a member of the Anglican Communion. The country has a long literary tradition and has contributed greatly to world literature.

Economy and the Land. Ireland's economy was agricultural until the 1950s, when a program of rapid industrialization began. This expansion has resulted in significant foreign investment, especially by the United States. Most of the Irish labor force is unionized. Agriculture continues to play an important role, however, and food is produced for both domestic consumption and trade. The country of Ireland occupies most of the island of Ireland but excludes Northern Ireland, which is part of the United Kingdom. The fertile central region features green, rolling hills, suitable for farming and pastureland, and is surrounded by coastal highlands. The climate is temperate maritime, with mild summers and winters and plentiful rainfall.

History and Politics. Around the fourth century B.C. Ireland's indigenous population was conquered by Gaels, a Celtic tribe, from continental Europe and Great Britain. Christianity was introduced by St. Patrick in A.D. 432, and periodic Viking raids began near the end of the eighth century. In the twelfth century the pope made the Norman king of England, Henry II, overlord of the island; the English intervened in a dispute between Irish kings; and centuries of British influence began. As British control grew, so did Irish Catholic hostility, arising from seizure of land by English settlers, the Protestant Reformation, and the elimination of political and religious freedoms. The Protestant majority of present-day Northern Ireland was established in the 1600s, when land taken from the Irish was distributed to English and Scottish Protestants. In 1801 the British Act of Union established the United Kingdom of Great Britain and Ireland. Religious freedom was regained in 1829, but the struggle for independence continued. Most of the Irish depended upon potatoes as a staple food, and hundreds of thousands died or emigrated in the 1840s when the crop failed because of a plant disease. Following an armed rebellion, the Irish Free State, a dominion of Great Britain, was created in 1921, with the predominantly Protestant countries in the north remaining under British rule. The nation became a republic in 1948. Many Irish citizens and Catholics in Northern Ireland continue to demand unification of the country, and the struggle occasionally erupts into violence. Neutrality remains the basis of foreign policy, and the nation is a strong supporter of European unity.   ■

ITALY

Official name Italian Republic
PEOPLE
Population 56,940,000. **Density** 490/mi² (189/km²). **Urban** 69%. **Capital** Rome, 2,830,569. **Ethnic groups**

Italian, others. **Languages** Italian. **Religions** Roman Catholic. **Life expectancy** 76 female, 72 male. **Literacy** 93%.

POLITICS
Government Republic. **Parties** Christian Democratic, Communist, Socialist, Social Movement. **Suffrage** Universal, over 18. **Memberships** NATO, OECD, UN. **Subdivisions** 20 regions.

ECONOMY
GNP $347,000,000,000. **Per capita** $5,314. **Monetary unit** Lira. **Trade partners** West Germany, France, Benelux countries, U.S., U.K. **Exports** Machinery, transportation equipment, textiles, food. **Imports** Machinery, transportation equipment, food, petroleum.

LAND
Description Southern Europe. **Area** 116,319 mi² (301,266 km²). **Highest point** Mt. Blanc (Monte Bianco), 15,771 ft (4,807 m). **Lowest point** Sea level.

People. Italy is populated mainly by Italian Roman Catholics. Most speak Italian; however, dialects often differ from region to region. Despite an ethnic homogeneity, the people exhibit diversity in terms of politics and culture. The country has about twelve political parties, and northern inhabitants are relatively prosperous, employed primarily in industry, whereas southerners are generally farmers and often poor. The birthplace of the Renaissance, Italy has made substantial contributions to world culture.

Economy and the Land. The Italian economy is based on private enterprise, although the government is involved in some industrial and commercial activities. Industry is centered in the north, producing steel, textiles, and chemicals. Much commercial agriculture is also based in the north, taking place on the rich soils of the Po Valley. A hilly terrain makes parts of the south unsuited for crop raising,

and livestock grazing is a main activity. Tourism is also an important contributor, with visitors drawn by the northern Alps, the sunny south, and the Italian cultural tradition. The island of Sicily, lying off the southwest coast, produces fruits, olives, and grapes. Sardinia, a western island, engages in some sheep and wheat raising. Except for the northern Po Valley, narrow areas along the coast, and a small section of the southern peninsula, Italy's terrain is mainly rugged and mountainous. The climate varies from cold in the Alps to mild and Mediterranean in other parts of the country.

History and Politics. Early influences in Italy included Greeks, Etruscans, and Celts. From the fifth century B.C. to the fifth century A.D., the dominant people were Romans descended from Sabines and neighboring Latins, who inhabited the Latium coast. Following the demise of the Roman Empire, rulers and influences included Byzantines; Lombards, an invading Germanic tribe; and the Frankish king Charlemagne, whom the pope crowned emperor of the Romans in 800. During the eleventh century, Italy became a region of city-states, and their cultural life led to the Renaissance, which started in the 1300s. As the city-states weakened, Italy fell victim to invasion and rule by France, Spain, and Austria, with these countries controlling various regions at different times. In 1861 Victor Emmanuel II, the king of Sardinia, proclaimed Italy a kingdom, and by 1871 the nation included the entire peninsula, with Rome as the capital and Victor Emmanuel as king. In 1922 Benito Mussolini, the leader of Italy's Fascist movement, came to power. By 1925 Mussolini was ruling as dictator, and an almost continuous period of warfare followed. In World War II the country allied with Germany, and a popular resistance movement evolved. The monarchy was ended by plebiscite in 1946, and the country became a republic. There are now many political parties, but the Christian Democratic, Communist, and Socialist parties are dominant. Italy's Communist party is the world's largest nonruling Communist party. ∎

LIECHTENSTEIN

Official name Principality of Liechtenstein
PEOPLE
Population 27,000. **Density** 435/mi² (169/km²). **Capital** Vaduz, 4,980. **Ethnic groups** Alemannic 95%, Italian and others 5%. **Languages** German. **Religions** Roman Catholic 83%, Protestant 7%. **Literacy** 100%.

POLITICS

Government Constitutional monarchy. **Parties** Fatherland Union, Progressive Citizens'. **Suffrage** Universal adult male, limited adult female. **Memberships** None. **Subdivisions** 11 communes.

ECONOMY

GDP $439,400,000. **Per capita** $16,900. **Monetary unit** Swiss franc. **Trade partners** Switzerland, other Western European countries. **Exports** Metal products, precision instruments, artificial teeth.

LAND

Description Central Europe, landlocked. **Area** 62 mi² (160 km²). **Highest point** Vorder-Grauspitz, 8,527 ft (2,599 m). **Lowest point** Ruggeller Riet, 1,411 ft (430 m).

People. In spite of its location at the crossroads of Europe, Liechtenstein has retained a largely homogeneous ethnicity. Almost all Liechtensteiners are descended from the Alemanni, a Germanic tribe, and many speak the Alemanni dialect. German, however, is the official language. Roman Catholicism is the most widely practiced religion but a Protestant minority also exists. Most of the country is mountainous, and population is concentrated on the fertile plains adjacent to the Rhine River, which forms the country's western boundary. Most Liechtensteiners work in factories or in trades.

Economy and the Land. The last few decades have seen the economy shift from agricultural to highly industrialized. Despite this growth in industry, Liechtenstein has not experienced a serious pollution problem, and the government continues its work to prevent the problem from occurring. An economic alliance with Switzerland dating from 1923 has been profoundly beneficial to Liechtenstein: the two nations form a customs union and use the same currency. Other important sources of revenue are tourism, the sale of postage stamps, and taxation of foreign businesses headquartered here. Most of Liechtenstein, one of the world's smallest nations, is covered by the Alps; nonetheless, its climate is mild.

History and Politics. Early inhabitants of what is now Liechtenstein included the Celts, Romans, and Alemanni, who arrived about A.D. 500. The area became part of the empire of the Frankish king Charlemagne in the late 700s, and following Charlemagne's death, it was divided into the lordships of Vaduz and Schellenberg. By 1719, when the state became part of the Holy Roman Empire, the Austrian House of Liechtenstein had purchased both lordships, uniting them as the Imperial Principality of Liechtenstein. The nation's independence dates from the abolition of the empire by France's Napoleon Bonaparte in 1806. Liechtenstein was neutral in both world wars and has remained unaffected by European conflicts. The government is a hereditary constitutional monarchy; the prince is the head of the House of Liechtenstein, thus chief of state, and the prime minister is the head of government. Women gained limited suffrage in 1984.   ■

LUXEMBOURG

Official name Grand Duchy of Luxembourg

PEOPLE

Population 365,000. **Density** 366/mi² (141/km²). **Urban** 78%. **Capital** Luxembourg, 78,924. **Ethnic groups** Mixed Celtic, French, and German. **Languages** Luxembourgish, French, German. **Religions** Roman Catholic 97%. **Life expectancy** 76 female, 71 male. **Literacy** 100%.

POLITICS

Government Constitutional monarchy. **Parties** Christian Socialist, Liberal, Socialist Workers'. **Suffrage** Universal, over 18. **Memberships** NATO, OECD, UN. **Subdivisions** 3 districts.

ECONOMY

GNP $3,400,000,000. **Per capita** $9,289. **Monetary unit** Franc. **Trade partners** West Germany, Belgium, France. **Exports** Steel, plastic, and rubber products. **Imports** Coal, petroleum, consumer goods.

LAND

Description Western Europe, landlocked. **Area** 998 mi² (2,586 km²). **Highest point** Buurgplaatz, 1,834 ft (559 m). **Lowest point** 427 ft (130 m).

People. Luxembourg's population bears the imprint of foreign influences, yet retains an individual character. Most Luxembourgers are a blend of Celtic, French, and German stock. German and French are official languages, as is Luxembourgish, an indigenous German dialect. Roman Catholicism is observed by virtually all the population. There are significant communities of guest workers from several European nations.

Economy and the Land. Luxembourg's steel industry forms the basis of its economy, and the country has compensated for a worldwide drop in the steel market by developing financial services, notably banking. Manufacturing of plastics and chemicals is also important, as is tourism. Luxembourg's trade benefits from the country's membership in the European Community and the Benelux union. Luxembourg has two distinct regions: the mountainous, wooded north and the open, rolling south, known as Bon Pays. The climate is temperate but somewhat cool and rainy.

History and Politics. The present city of Luxembourg developed from a castle built in A.D. 963 by Count Siegfried of Ardennes. Several heavily fortified towns grew up around the castle, and the area became known as the Gibraltar of the North because of those fortifications. The duchy remained semiautonomous until the Burgundians conquered the area in 1443. Various European powers ruled Luxembourg for most of the next four centuries, and in 1815 the duchy was elevated to a grand duchy. It became autonomous in 1839 and was recognized in 1867 as an independent state. Despite its declaration of neutrality, Luxembourg was occupied by Germany in both world wars. The country maintains a pro-Western, pan-European stance in its foreign relations. ∎

MALTA

Official name Republic of Malta

PEOPLE

Population 360,000. **Density** 2,951/mi² (1,139/km²). **Urban** 83%. **Capital** Valletta, 13,962. **Ethnic groups** Mixed Arab, Sicilian, Norman, Spanish, Italian, English. **Languages** Maltese, English. **Religions** Roman Catholic 98%. **Life expectancy** 74 female, 70 male. **Literacy** 83%.

POLITICS

Government Republic. **Parties** Labor, Nationalist. **Suffrage** Universal, over 18. **Memberships** CW, UN. **Subdivisions** 13 electoral districts.

ECONOMY

GDP $1,140,000,000. **Per capita** $3,499. **Monetary unit** Pound. **Trade partners** West Germany, Italy, U.K. **Exports** Clothing, textiles, petroleum products. **Imports** Manufactured goods, machinery, food, petroleum.

LAND

Description Mediterranean island. **Area** 122 mi² (316 km²). **Highest point** 829 ft (253 m). **Lowest point** Sea level.

People. Malta's diverse population reflects centuries of rule by Arabs, Normans, and the British. The official languages are English and Maltese, the latter a blend of Arabic and a Sicilian dialect of Italian. Roman Catholicism is practiced by the majority of residents. Malta is one of the world's most densely populated nations.

Economy and the Land. Situated strategically between Europe and Africa, Malta became an important military site for foreign powers with the opening of the Suez Canal in 1869. Its economy was thus shaped by the patterns of war and peace in the Mediterranean but has recently turned toward commercial shipbuilding, construction, manufacturing, and tourism. Its soil is poor and rocky, and most food is imported. Although there are many natural harbors and hundreds of miles of coastline, fishing is not a major source of income. Malta, with its hilly terrain, is subtropical in summer and temperate the rest of the year.

History and Politics. The Phoenicians and Carthaginians first colonized the island of Malta between 1000 and 600 B.C. Malta was made part of the Roman and Byzantine empires and then was ruled successively by Arabs, Normans, and various feudal lords. In the 1500s the Holy Roman Emperor Charles V ceded Malta to the Knights of St. John of Jerusalem, an order of the Roman Catholic church. The Knights' reign, marked by cultural and architectural achievements, ended with surrender to France's Napoleon Bonaparte in 1798. The Maltese resisted French rule, however, and offered control to Britain, becoming part of the United Kingdom in 1814. Throughout the two world wars Malta was a vital naval base for the Allied forces. It achieved independence from Britain in 1964 and became a republic ten years later. In 1979 the last British and North Atlantic Treaty Organization (NATO) military forces departed, and Malta declared its neutrality and nonalignment. ▪

MONACO

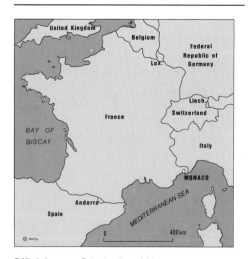

Official name Principality of Monaco
PEOPLE
Population 28,000. **Density** 46,667/mi² (18,667/km²). **Urban** 100%. **Capital** Monaco, 25,000. **Ethnic groups** French 58%, Monegasque 19%, Italian 17%. **Languages** French, Monegasque, Italian, English. **Religions** Roman Catholic 95%. **Literacy** 99%.

POLITICS
Government Constitutional monarchy. **Parties** National and Democratic Union, Socialist. **Suffrage** Universal adult. **Memberships** None.
ECONOMY
Monetary Unit French franc.
LAND
Description Southern Europe. **Area** 0.6 mi² (1.5 km²). **Highest point** 459 ft (140 m). **Lowest point** Sea level.

People. Monaco is inhabited mostly by French citizens. Monegasques, citizens of indigenous descent, and Italians form the rest of the population. Many foreigners have taken up residence, drawn by the country's tax benefits. French is the official language. Monegasque, a blend of French and Italian, is also spoken, as are Italian and English. Most residents are Roman Catholic.

Economy and the Land. Monaco's beautiful seaside location, mild Mediterranean climate, and famous gambling casino in Monte Carlo make it a popular tourist haven. Consequently, tourism forms the backbone of the economy. Production of chemicals, food products, and perfumes, among other light industries, are additional sources of income. Monaco also profits from many foreign businesses, attracted by the favorable tax climate, that are headquartered in the principality. France and Monaco form a customs union for a mutually beneficial trade system; the French franc is Monaco's official currency. The world's second smallest independent state in area—after Vatican City—Monaco has four regions: the old city of Monaco-Ville, site of the royal palace; Monte Carlo, the resort and major tourist center; La Condamine, the port area; and Fontvieille, the rapidly growing industrial section.

History and Politics. Known to the Phoenicians, Greeks, and Romans, the region became a Genoese colony in the twelfth century A.D. Around the turn of the fourteenth century, the area was granted to the Grimaldi family of Genoa. France, Spain, and Sardinia had intermittent control of Monaco from 1400 until 1861, when its autonomy was recognized by the Franco-Monegasque Treaty. Another treaty, providing for French protection of Monaco, was signed in 1918. The absolute rule of Monaco's princes ended with the 1911 constitution. ▪

NETHERLANDS

Official name Kingdom of the Netherlands
PEOPLE
Population 14,465,000. **Density** 910/mi² (351/km²). **Urban** 88%. **Capital** Amsterdam (constitutional),

687,397; The Hague (seat of government), 449,338.
Ethnic groups Dutch 99%, Indonesian and others 1%.
Languages Dutch. **Religions** Roman Catholic 40%,
Protestant 31%. **Life expectancy** 78 female, 74 male.
Literacy 99%.

POLITICS
Government Constitutional monarchy. **Parties** Christian
Democratic Appeal, Democrats '66, Labor, Liberal.
Suffrage Universal, over 18. **Memberships** NATO,
OECD, UN. **Subdivisions** 16 provinces.

ECONOMY
GNP $137,300,000,000. **Per capita** $9,807. **Monetary
unit** Guilder. **Trade partners** West Germany, Belgium,
France, U.S., U.K. **Exports** Food, machinery, chemicals,
petroleum products. **Imports** Machinery, petroleum,
transportation equipment, food.

LAND
Description Western Europe. **Area** 15,892 mi² (41,160
km²). **Highest point** 1,053 ft (321 m). **Lowest point**
Prins Alexander polder, 22 ft (6.7 m) below sea level.

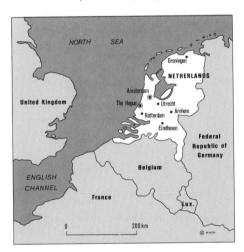

People. The major ethnic group is the Dutch, for
the most part a mixture of Germanic peoples.
There are small minorities from the former Dutch
possessions of Indonesia and Suriname. Dutch is
the official language, but many Netherlanders also
speak English or German. Although most Dutch are
Christian, the nation has a history of religious
tolerance that has drawn countless refugees.

Economy and the Land. A variety of manufacturing strengths—notably the metal, chemical, and
food-processing industries—fuels the prosperous
economy. Tourism and the production of natural
gas are also important. A lack of natural resources
obliges the Netherlands to import many goods. The
country benefits from its strategic position and has
enjoyed success in shipping and trade. Much of the
Netherlands, including most farmland, has been

reclaimed from the sea through artificial drainage.
The land is almost uniformly flat, and proximity to
the sea produces a mild, damp climate. The Kingdom of the Netherlands includes the Netherland
Antilles, two groups of Caribbean islands.

History and Politics. The Germanic tribes of the
area were conquered in 58 B.C. by the Romans,
who were driven out in the A.D. 400s by the Franks.
As part of the Low Countries with Belgium and
Luxembourg, the Netherlands was dominated successively by Charlemagne, the dukes of Burgundy,
the Hapsburgs, and rulers of Spain. Spanish persecution of Dutch Protestants led to a revolt that in
1581 created the Republic of the United Netherlands. In the 1600s the Netherlands became a
maritime as well as a colonial power and produced
many masterpieces in painting. But a series of wars
with England and France ending in 1714 spelled
the end of Dutch influence, and the nation fell to
France in 1795. With the defeat of Napoleon Bonaparte of France in 1815, the Netherlands was
united with Belgium and became an independent
kingdom. Belgium seceded in 1830. The Netherlands declared its neutrality in both world wars but
was occupied by Germany from 1940 to 1945. The
war cost the country many lives and much of its
economic strength. Membership in several international economic unions aided recovery. Since the
war the Netherlands has abandoned neutrality and
now maintains a pro-Western stance in foreign
affairs. ∎

NORWAY

Official name Kingdom of Norway
PEOPLE
Population 4,150,000. **Density** 28/mi² (11/km²). **Urban**
70%. **Capital** Oslo, 448,747. **Ethnic groups** Germanic,
Lappish. **Languages** Norwegian, Lappish. **Religions**
Lutheran 94%. **Life expectancy** 79 female, 74 male.
Literacy 100%.

POLITICS
Government Constitutional monarchy. **Parties** Center,
Christian People's, Conservative, Labor, Progressive,
Socialist Left. **Suffrage** Universal, over 18.
Memberships NATO, OECD, UN. **Subdivisions** 19
counties.

ECONOMY
GNP $56,200,000,000. **Per capita** $13,600. **Monetary
unit** Krone. **Trade partners** U.K., West Germany,
Sweden, U.S. **Exports** Petroleum, natural gas, metals,
paper and wood pulp, chemicals, fish products. **Imports**
Machinery, transportation equipment, food, iron and
steel, textiles, clothing.

LAND
Description Northern Europe. **Area** 149,158 mi² (386,317 km²). **Highest point** Glittertinden, 8,110 ft (2,472 m). **Lowest point** Sea level.

People. Because of its relatively remote location in far northern Europe, Norway has seen few population migrations and possesses a virtually homogeneous population, which is predominantly Germanic, Norwegian speaking, and Lutheran. Small communities of Lapps and Finns live in the far north, while most Norwegians live in the south and along the coast. Two mutually intelligible forms of the Norwegian language are taught in schools.

Economy and the Land. Norway's economy, based on shipping, trade, and the mining of offshore oil and natural gas, takes its shape from the nation's proximity to several seas. Shipbuilding, fishing, and forestry are also important activities. Norway is a leading producer of hydroelectricity. Combined with some government control of the economy, these lucrative activities have given the nation a high standard of living and fairly low unemployment. Most of Norway is a high plateau covered with mountains. The Gulf Stream gives the nation a much milder climate than other places at the same latitude.

History and Politics. Parts of present-day Norway were inhabited by about 9000 B.C. Germanic tribes began immigrating to the area about 2000 B.C. Between A.D. 800 and 1100 Viking ships from Norway raided coastal towns throughout Western Europe and also colonized Greenland and Iceland. Unified around 900, Norway was subsequently shaken by civil war, plague, and the end of its royal line. It entered a union with Denmark in 1380, becoming a Danish province in 1536. Around the end of the Napoleonic Wars, in 1814, Norway became part of Sweden. A long struggle against Swedish rule ended in 1905 as Sweden recognized Norwegian independence, and a Danish prince was made king. Norway was neutral in World War I but endured German occupation during World War II. In 1967 the government initiated a wide-ranging social-welfare system. Norway retains relations with Western nations and the Soviet Union but does not allow foreign military bases or nuclear arms on its soil. ∎

POLAND

Official name Polish People's Republic
PEOPLE
Population 37,055,000. **Density** 307/mi² (119/km²). **Urban** 59%. **Capital** Warsaw, 1,628,900. **Ethnic groups** Polish 99%. **Languages** Polish. **Religions** Roman Catholic 95%. **Life expectancy** 75 female, 70 male. **Literacy** 98%.
POLITICS
Government Socialist republic. **Parties** United Workers'. **Suffrage** Universal, over 18. **Memberships** CEMA, UN, Warsaw Pact. **Subdivisions** 49 provinces.
ECONOMY
GNP $186,800,000,000. **Per capita** $5,160. **Monetary unit** Złoty. **Trade partners** U.S.S.R., Eastern European countries, West Germany. **Exports** Machinery, equipment, fuels, manufactured goods, textiles, food. **Imports** Machinery, petroleum, raw materials, food.
LAND
Description Eastern Europe. **Area** 120,728 mi² (312,683 km²). **Highest point** Rysy, 8,199 ft (2,499 m). **Lowest point** Raczki Elbląskie, 5.9 ft (1.8 m) below sea level.

People. Poland's homogeneous population is partially a result of Nazi persecution during World War II, which virtually obliterated the Jewish community and led to the emigration of most minorities. Roman Catholicism, practiced by almost all Poles, remains a unifying force. The urban population has risen in the postwar period because of government emphasis on industrialization.

Economy and the Land. Government policies since the war have transformed Poland from an agricultural nation into an industrial one. It is a leading producer of coal and has several metal-processing industries. Machinery and textiles are important products. Although most industries are government controlled, the majority of farms are privately owned. Poland's poor soil and short growing season have kept it from achieving agricultural self-sufficiency. Shortages in consumer goods have been chronic since the 1970s, when debts to the West were compounded by the failure of Polish goods in world markets. Poland has a mostly flat terrain—except for mountains in the south—and a temperate climate.

History and Politics. Slavic tribes inhabited the region of modern Poland several thousand years ago. The Piast dynasty began in the A.D. 900s and established Roman Catholicism as the official religion. In the sixteenth century the Jagiellonian dynasty guided the empire to its height of expansion. A subsequent series of upheavals and wars weakened Poland, and from the 1770s to the 1790s it was partitioned three times, finally disappearing as an independent state. In 1918, following the Allies' World War I victory, Poland regained its independence and, through the 1919 Treaty of Versailles, much of its former territory. World War II began with Germany's invasion of Poland in 1939. With the end of the war Poland came under Communist control and Soviet domination. Antigovernment strikes and riots, some spurred by rising food prices, erupted periodically, and following the formation of the trade union Solidarity, the government imposed martial law in 1981. Although martial law was lifted in 1982, many restrictions and tensions remain.   ∎

PORTUGAL

Official name Portuguese Republic
PEOPLE
Population 10,065,000. **Density** 283/mi² (109/km²).
Urban 30%. **Capital** Lisbon, 807,200. **Ethnic groups**
Mediterranean, African. **Languages** Portuguese.
Religions Roman Catholic 97%. **Life expectancy** 75 female, 70 male. **Literacy** 80%.
POLITICS
Government Republic. **Parties** Communist, Social Democratic, Social Democratic Center, Socialist.
Suffrage Universal, over 18. **Memberships** EC, NATO, OECD, UN. **Subdivisions** 18 districts, 2 autonomous regions.
ECONOMY
GNP $23,400,000,000. **Per capita** $2,328. **Monetary unit** Escudo. **Trade partners** U.K., West Germany, other Western European countries, U.S. **Exports** Clothing, textiles, cork and cork products, wood, food and wine.
Imports Petroleum, industrial machinery, transportation equipment, cotton, chemicals.
LAND
Description Southern Europe. **Area** 35,516 mi² (91,985 km²). **Highest point** Pico Pt., 7,713 ft (2,351 m). **Lowest point** Sea level.

People. Although many invaders have been drawn by Portugal's long coastline throughout past centuries, today the population is relatively homogeneous. One group of invaders, the Romans, laid the basis for the chief language, Portuguese, which developed from Latin. The only significant minority is composed of black Africans from former colonies. Most Portuguese are rural and belong to the Roman Catholic church, which has had a strong influence on society.

Economy and the Land. The mainstays of agriculture and fishing were joined in the mid-1900s by manufacturing, chiefly of textiles, clothing, cork products, metals, and machinery. A variety of social and political ills have contributed to Portugal's status as one of Europe's poorest nations: past wars with African colonies, an influx of colonial refugees, and intraparty violence. Tourism has declined slightly, and agriculture has suffered from outdated techniques and a rural-to-urban population shift. The terrain is mostly plains and lowlands, with some mountains; the climate is mild and sunny.

History and Politics. Inhabited by an Iberian people about five thousand years ago, the area was later visited by Phoenicians, Celts, and Greeks before falling to the Romans around the first century B.C. The Romans were followed by Germanic Visigoths and in A.D. 711 by North African Muslims, who greatly influenced Portuguese art and architecture. Spain absorbed Portugal in 1094, and Portugal declared its independence in 1143. About one hundred years later the last of the Muslims were expelled. Portugal's golden age—during which its navigators explored the globe and founded colonies in South America, Africa, and the Far East—lasted from 1385 to the late 1500s. Rival European powers soon began to seize Portuguese holdings, and in 1580 Spain invaded Portugal, ruling until 1640, when the Spanish were driven out and independence reestablished. After the 1822 loss of Brazil, Portugal's most valuable colony, and decades of opposition, a weakened monarchy was overthrown in 1910. The subsequent parliamentary democracy, marked by rapid power shifts and economic instability, proved a failure, and in 1926 it gave way to a military coup. Antonio Salazar became prime minister in 1932, ruling as a virtual dictator until 1968. Salazar's favored treatment of the rich and his refusal to relinquish Portugal's colonies aggravated the economic situation. A 1974 coup toppled Salazar's successor and set up a military government, events that sparked violence among political parties. Almost all Portuguese colonies gained independence during the next two years. A democratic government was adopted in 1976, and since then the nation has been ruled by differing coalitions. Portugal has close ties to the West and has sought to improve relations with the Third World. ∎

ROMANIA

Official name Socialist Republic of Romania
PEOPLE
Population 22,860,000. **Density** 249/mi² (96/km²).
Urban 50%. **Capital** Bucharest, 1,929,360. **Ethnic groups** Romanian 88%, Hungarian 8%. **Languages** Romanian. **Religions** Romanian Orthodox 80%, Roman Catholic 6%. **Life expectancy** 74 female, 69 male. **Literacy** 98%.

POLITICS
Government Socialist republic. **Parties** Communist. **Suffrage** Universal, over 18. **Memberships** CEMA, UN, Warsaw Pact. **Subdivisions** 40 counties, 1 municipality.
ECONOMY
GNP $104,800,000,000. **Per capita** $4,238. **Monetary unit** Leu. **Trade partners** U.S.S.R., West Germany, East Germany. **Exports** Machinery, fuels, textiles, wood products, food. **Imports** Machinery, fuels, iron ore, motor vehicles.

LAND
Description Eastern Europe. **Area** 91,699 mi² (237,500 km²). **Highest point** Moldoveanu, 8,343 ft (2,543 m). **Lowest point** Sea level.

People. The majority population of Romania belongs to the Romanian Orthodox church and traces its roots to Latin-speaking Romans, Thracians, Slavs, and Celts. Minorities, concentrated in Transylvania and areas north and west of Bucharest, are mainly Roman Catholic Hungarians and Germans. Other minorities include Gypsies, Serbs, Croats, Ukrainians, Greeks, Turks, and Armenians. Almost all inhabitants speak Romanian, although other languages are often spoken by minority groups.

Economy and the Land. When Romania became a Communist country in the 1940s, the government began programs to turn the country from agriculture to industry. The economy is now based on industry, and products include oil, wood, and natural gas. Although Romania remains less developed than many other European countries, it has experienced post-war growth in its gross national product. Most agriculture is collectivized, and corn and wheat are major crops. The terrain is marked by a low-lying south-to-northeast plateau that curves around several mountain ranges, including the Carpathians, found in the northern and central regions. The climate is continental, with cold, snowy winters and warm summers.

History and Politics. First colonized by the Dacians, a Thracian tribe, around the fourth century B.C., the area became the Roman province of Romania in the second century A.D. Invading Bulgars, Goths, Huns, Magyars, Slavs, and Tartars followed the Romans. Between 1250 and 1350 the independent Romanian principalities of Walachia and Moldavia emerged. In the fifteenth and sixteenth centuries Ottoman Turks conquered the principalities, and following a Russian-Turkish war, Russians occupied the states. In 1861 Walachia and Moldavia were united as Romania, in 1878 they gained independence, and in 1881 Romania was proclaimed a kingdom. The nation's government was marked by oppression and a concentration of land and wealth among the aristocracy, and a 1907 rebellion was quelled by the army. In 1919, after a World War I alliance with the Allies, Romania gained Transylvania and other territories. Instability and dissatisfaction, spurred by worldwide economic depression, continued through the 1930s. With the cooperation of Romanian leadership, Germany occupied the country in World War II. In 1944 Soviet troops entered Romania, and the nation subsequently joined the Allies. A Communist government was established in 1945, and in 1947 the king was forced to abdicate and Romania officially became a Communist country. Initially Romania's policies were closely tied to those of the Soviet Union, but renewed nationalism in the sixties led to several independent policy decisions. ∎

SAN MARINO

Official name Republic of San Marino
PEOPLE
Population 23,000. **Density** 958/mi² (377/km²). **Urban** 74%. **Capital** San Marino, 4,623. **Ethnic groups** San Marinese. **Languages** Italian. **Religions** Roman Catholic. **Literacy** 97%.
POLITICS
Government Republic. **Parties** Christian Democratic, Communist, Socialist, Unitary Socialist. **Suffrage** Universal adult. **Memberships** None. **Subdivisions** 9 castles.
ECONOMY
Monetary unit Italian lira. **Trade partners** Italy. **Exports** Construction materials, textiles, wine, postage stamps. **Imports** Consumer goods, petroleum, gold.
LAND
Description Southern Europe, landlocked. **Area** 24 mi² (61 km²). **Highest point** Monte Titano, 2,425 ft (739 m). **Lowest point** 174 ft (53 m).

People. San Marino is completely surrounded by Italy; thus the San Marinese are ethnically similar to Italians, combining Mediterranean, Alpine, Adriatic, and Nordic roots. Italian is the main language, and Roman Catholicism the major religion. Despite San Marino's similarities to Italy, its long tradition of independence has given its citizens a strong national identity.

Economy and the Land. San Marino and Italy's close economic relationship has resulted in a mutually beneficial customs union; San Marino has no customs restrictions at its borders and receives annual budget subsidiary payments from Italy. Most San Marinese are employed in agriculture; livestock raising is a main activity, and crops include wheat and grapes. Tourism and the sale of postage stamps are major economic contributors, as is industry, which produces construction materials and textiles for export. Located in the Apennine Mountains, San Marino has a rugged terrain and a generally moderate climate.

History and Politics. San Marino is considered the world's oldest republic. Tradition has it that Marinus, a Christian stonecutter seeking religious freedom in a time of repressive Roman rule, founded the state in the fourth century A.D. Partly because of the protection afforded by its mountainous terrain, San Marino has been able maintain continuous independence despite attempted invasions. In the 1300s the country became a republic, and the pope recognized its independent status in 1631. San Marino signed its first treaty of friendship with Italy in 1862. In its foreign relations, the country maintains a distinct identity and status. ∎

SOVIET UNION

Official name Union of Soviet Socialist Republics
PEOPLE
Population 275,590,000. **Density** 32/mi² (12/km²).
Urban 64%. **Capital** Moscow, 8,202,000. **Ethnic groups**
Russian 52%, Ukrainian 16%, others 32%. **Languages**
Russian; other Slavic, Altaic, and Indo-European
languages. **Religions** Russian Orthodox 18%, Muslim
9%. **Life expectancy** 75 female, 70 male. **Literacy** 100%.
POLITICS
Government Socialist republic. **Parties** Communist.
Suffrage Universal, over 18. **Memberships** CEMA, UN,
Warsaw Pact. **Subdivisions** 15 Soviet Socialist
Republics.
ECONOMY
GNP $1,715,000,000,000. **Per capita** $6,352. **Monetary
unit** Ruble. **Trade partners** Eastern European countries,
Finland, West Germany, France. **Exports** Petroleum,
petroleum products, natural gas, machinery,
manufactured goods, metals. **Imports** Food, machinery,
steel products, consumer goods.
LAND
Description Eastern Europe and northern Asia. **Area**
8,600,383 mi² (22,274,900 km²). **Highest point**
Communism Pk., 24,590 ft (7,495 m). **Lowest point**
Vpadina Karagiye, 433 ft (132 m) below sea level.

People. The varied population of the Soviet Union
is composed of more than one hundred distinct
groups. Nearly three-quarters of the people are
Eastern Slavs, and more than 70 percent of this
group are Russians. The remaining Slavs are
Ukrainians and Belorussians. The rest of the population belongs to Turkic, Finno-Ugric, Caucasian,
other Indo-European groups, and a mixture of

peoples including Inuit. Each group speaks its own
language, although Russian is the most widely
used. Religious practice is discouraged by the
state, and churches have no legal status, although
Russian Orthodox, Islam, Catholicism, Protestant-
ism, and other religions are actively practiced.

Economy and the Land. As an industrial power,
the Soviet Union ranks second only to the United
States. Mining, steel production, and other heavy
industries predominate. The economy is controlled
by the state, and economic policies are adminis-
tered through a series of five-year plans, which
emphasize industrial and technological growth. The
Soviet economy is suffering from low productivity,
energy shortages, and a lack of skilled labor,
problems the government hopes can be alleviated
by increased use of technology and science. The
Soviet Union trades primarily with members of the
Council for Mutual Economic Assistance
(COMECON), although trade with the West has
risen sharply in the past few years. Geographically,
the Soviet Union is the largest nation in the world.
Its terrain is widely varied and richly endowed with
minerals. Though the country contains some of the
world's most fertile land, long winters and hot, dry
summers keep many crop yields low.

History and Politics. Inhabited as early as the
Stone Age, what is now the Soviet Union was much
later invaded successively by Scythians, Sarmati-
ans, Goths, Huns, Bulgars, Slavs, and others. By
A.D. 989 Byzantine cultural influence had become
predominant. Various groups and regions were
slowly incorporated into a single state. In 1547 Ivan
IV was crowned czar of all Russia, beginning a
tradition of czarist rule that lasted until the 1917
Russian Revolution, when the Bolsheviks came to
power and named Vladimir Ilyich Lenin as head of
the first Soviet government. The Bolsheviks established a Communist state and weathered a bitter
civil war. Joseph Stalin succeeded Lenin as head of
state in 1924 and initiated a series of political
purges that lasted through the 1930s. The Soviet
Union became embroiled in World War II, siding
with the Allies, losing over twenty million people,
and suffering widespread destruction of its cities
and countryside. It emerged from the war with
extended influence, however, having annexed part
of Finland and several Eastern European nations.
Following Stalin's death in 1953, the Soviet Union
experienced a liberalization of policies under Nikita
Krushchev. In 1964 Leonid Brezhnev worked to
consolidate and strengthen the power of the Secre-
tariat and Politburo of the Communist party. Mikhail
S. Gorbachev, the youngest Soviet leader in decades, took office in 1985.   ■

SPAIN

Official name Spanish State
PEOPLE
Population 38,515,000. **Density** 198/mi² (76/km²).
Urban 91%. **Capital** Madrid, 3,188,297. **Ethnic groups**
Mixed Mediterranean and Nordic. **Languages** Spanish.
Religions Roman Catholic 99%. **Life expectancy** 76
female, 72 male. **Literacy** 97%.
POLITICS
Government Constitutional monarchy. **Parties** Popular
Alliance, Popular Democratic, Socialist Workers'.
Suffrage Universal, over 18. **Memberships** NATO,
OECD, UN. **Subdivisions** 17 autonomous regions.
ECONOMY
GNP $179,700,000,000. **Per capita** $4,746. **Monetary
unit** Peseta. **Trade partners** France, U.S., West
Germany, Italy, U.K. **Exports** Iron and steel products,
machinery, food, automobiles, footwear. **Imports** Fuels,
machinery, chemicals, iron and steel, food.
LAND
Description Southern Europe. **Area** 194,882 mi²
(504,741 km²). **Highest point** Pico de Teide, Tenerife,
Canary Is., 12,198 ft (3,718 m). **Lowest point** Sea level.

People. The population of Spain is a mixture of
ethnic groups from northern Europe and the area
surrounding the Mediterranean Sea. Spanish is the
official language; however, several regional dialects of Spanish are commonly spoken. The
Basque minority, one of the oldest surviving ethnic
groups in Europe, lives mainly in the Pyrenees in
northern Spain, preserving its own language and
traditions. Since the 1978 constitution, Spain has
not had an official religion, yet nearly all its people
are Roman Catholic. Spain has a rich artistic
tradition, blending Moorish and Western cultures.

Economy and the Land. Despite the effects of the
general worldwide recession of the 1970s, Spain
has benefited greatly from an economic-
restructuring program that began in the 1950s. The
nation has concentrated on developing industry,
which now employs over 30 percent of the population. Exploitation of natural-gas deposits is also
being explored, with the hope of reducing Spain's
dependence on oil imports. The agricultural contri-
bution to the economy has declined to about half of
peak production and employment. Spain's terrain is
mainly composed of a dry plateau area; mountains
cover the northern section, and plains extend down
the country's eastern coast. Climate in the eastern
and southern regions is Mediterranean, while the
northwest has more rainfall and less sunshine
throughout the year.

History and Politics. Spain is among the oldest
inhabited regions in Europe. For centuries a Roman
province, Spain was conquered by the Visigoths in
the A.D. 500s, only to change hands again in the
700s when the Arab-Berbers, or Moors, seized
control of all but a narrow strip of northern Spain.
Christian kings reclaimed the country from the
eleventh to the fourteenth centuries. Spain, controlled by the three kingdoms of Navarre, Aragon,
and Castile, was united in the late 1400s under
King Ferdinand and Queen Isabella. At the height
of its empire, Spain claimed territory in North and
South America, northern Africa, Italy, and the Canary Islands. However, a series of wars burdened
Spain financially, and in the 1500s, under King
Philip II, the country entered a period of decline.
Throughout the 1700s and 1800s, the nation lost
most of its colonial possessions through treaty or
revolution. In 1936 a bitter civil war erupted between factions supporting the monarchy and those
wishing to establish a republic. General Francisco
Franco, leader of the successful monarchist army,
ruled as dictator of Spain from the end of the war
until his death in 1975. Spain enjoyed phenomenal
economic growth during the 1950s and 1960s;
however, that growth declined in the 1970s. Since
Franco's death, King Juan Carlos has led the
country toward a more democratic form of government. ∎

SWEDEN

Official name Kingdom of Sweden
PEOPLE
Population 8,335,000. **Density** 48/mi² (19/km²). **Urban**

83%. **Capital** Stockholm, 649,686. **Ethnic groups**
Swedish, Lappish. **Languages** Swedish. **Religions**
Lutheran 94%. **Life expectancy** 79 female, 75 male.
Literacy 99%.

POLITICS

Government Constitutional monarchy. **Parties** Center,
Communist, Moderate Coalition, People's, Social
Democratic. **Suffrage** Universal, over 18. **Memberships**
OECD, UN. **Subdivisions** 24 counties.

ECONOMY

GDP $81,000,000,000. **Per capita** $10,285. **Monetary
unit** Krona. **Trade partners** West Germany, U.K.,
Norway, U.S., Denmark, Finland. **Exports** Machinery,
motor vehicles, wood pulp, paper products, iron and
steel products. **Imports** Machinery, petroleum,
petroleum products, chemicals, food.

LAND

Description Northern Europe. **Area** 173,780 mi²
(450,089 km²). **Highest point** Kebnekaise, 6,926 ft
(2,111 m). **Lowest point** Sea level.

People. The most significant minorities in the largely urban Swedish population are Swedes of Finnish
origin and a small number of Lapps. Sweden is also
the home of immigrants from other Nordic countries
and Yugoslavia, Greece, and Turkey. Swedish is
the main language, although Finns and Lapps often
speak other tongues. English is the leading foreign
language, especially among students and younger
people.

Economy and the Land. Sweden has one of the
highest standards of living in the world. Taxes are
also high, but the government provides exceptional
benefits for most citizens, including free education
and medical care, pension payments, four-week
vacations, and payments for child care. The nation
is industrial and bases its economy on its three
most important natural resources—timber, iron

ore, and water power. More than a fourth of its
exports are lumber or wood products. The iron and
steel industry produces high-quality steel used in
ball bearings, precision tools, agricultural machinery, aircraft, automobiles, and ships. Swedish farmers rely heavily on dairy products and livestock, and
most farms are part of Sweden's agricultural-
cooperative movement. Sweden's varied terrain
includes mountains, forests, plains, and sandy
beaches. The climate is temperate, with cold winters in the north. Northern Sweden lies in the Land
of the Midnight Sun and experiences periods of
twenty-four hours of daylight in summer and darkness in winter.

History and Politics. Inhabitants of what is now
Sweden began to trade with the Roman Empire
about 50 B.C. Successful sailing expeditions by
Swedish Vikings began about A.D. 800. In the
fourteenth century the kingdom came under Danish
rule but left the union in 1523 and declared its
independence. The Swedish king offered protection
to the followers of Martin Luther, and Lutheranism
was soon declared the state religion. By the late
1660s Sweden had become one of the great powers of Europe; it suffered a military defeat by Russia
in 1709, however, and gradually lost most of its
European possessions. An 1809 constitution gave
most of the executive power of the government to
the king. Despite this, the power of the Parliament
gradually increased, and parliamentary rule was
adopted in 1917. A 1975 constitution reduced the
king's role to a ceremonial one. Sweden remained
neutral during both world wars.   ■

SWITZERLAND

Official name Swiss Confederation

PEOPLE

Population 6,485,000. **Density** 408/mi² (157/km²).
Urban 58%. **Capital** Bern, 145,300. **Ethnic groups**
German 65%, French 18%, Italian 10%, Romansch 1%.
Languages German, French, Italian. **Religions** Roman
Catholic 49%, Protestant 48%. **Life expectancy** 78
female, 74 male. **Literacy** 99%.

POLITICS

Government Republic. **Parties** Christian Democratic
People's, People's, Radical Democratic, Social
Democratic. **Suffrage** Universal, over 20. **Memberships**
OECD. **Subdivisions** 26 cantons.

ECONOMY

GNP $95,600,000,000. **Per capita** $14,270. **Monetary unit** Franc. **Trade partners** West Germany, France, Italy, U.S., U.K. **Exports** Machinery, electric appliances, chemicals, precision instruments, watches, textiles. **Imports** Machinery, metals and metal products, petroleum, motor vehicles, iron and steel, food, chemicals.

LAND

Description Central Europe, landlocked. **Area** 15,943 mi² (41,293 km²). **Highest point** Monte Rosa (Dufourspitze), 15,203 ft (4,634 m). **Lowest point** Lago Maggiore, 633 ft (193 m).

People. About seven hundred years ago, the Swiss began joining together for mutual defense but were able to preserve their regional differences in language and customs. The country has three official languages—German, French, and Italian—and a fourth language, Romansch, is spoken by a minority. Dialects often differ from community to community. The population is concentrated on a central plain located between mountain ranges.

Economy and the Land. The Alps and Jura Mountains cover nearly 70 percent of Switzerland, making much of the land unsuited for agriculture but providing the basis for a thriving tourist industry. The central plain contains rich cropland and holds Switzerland's major cities and manufacturing facilities, many specializing in high-quality, precision products. Switzerland is also an international banking and finance center. Straddling the ranges of the central Alps, Switzerland has a terrain of mountains, hills, and plateaus. The climate is temperate but varies with altitude.

History and Politics. Helvetic Celts inhabited the area of present-day Switzerland when Julius Cae-

sar conquered the region, annexing it to the Roman Empire. As the Roman Empire declined, northern and western Germanic tribes began a series of invasions, and in the 800s the region became part of the empire of the Frankish king Charlemagne. In 1291 leaders of the three Swiss cantons, or regions, signed an agreement declaring their freedom and promising mutual aid against any foreign ruler. The confederation was the beginning of modern Switzerland. Over the next few centuries Switzerland became a military power, expanding its territories until 1515, when it was defeated by France. Soon after, Switzerland adopted a policy of permanent neutrality. The country was again conquered by France during the French Revolution; however, after Napoleon's final defeat in 1815, the Congress of Vienna guaranteed Switzerland's neutrality, a guarantee that has never been broken. ∎

TURKEY

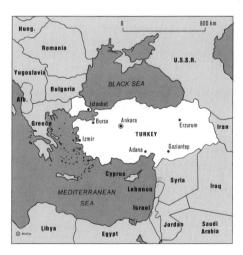

Official name Republic of Turkey

PEOPLE

Population 50,730,000. **Density** 169/mi² (65/km²). **Urban** 45%. **Capital** Ankara, 1,877,755. **Ethnic groups** Turkish 85%, Kurdish 12%. **Languages** Turkish, Kurdish. **Religions** Muslim 98%. **Life expectancy** 64 female, 60 male. **Literacy** 70%.

POLITICS
Government Republic. **Parties** Motherland, Nationalist Democracy, Populist. **Suffrage** Universal, over 21. **Memberships** NATO, OECD, UN. **Subdivisions** 67 provinces.

ECONOMY
GNP $53,800,000,000. **Per capita** $1,096. **Monetary unit** Lira. **Trade partners** Iraq, West Germany, U.S., Libya, other Western European countries. **Exports** Cotton, tobacco, fruits, nuts, food, textiles. **Imports** Petroleum, machinery, transportation equipment, metals, fertilizer.

LAND
Description Southeastern Europe and southwestern Asia. **Area** 300,948 mi² (779,452 km²). **Highest point** Mt. Ararat, 16,804 ft (5,122 m). **Lowest point** Sea level.

People. Turkey's majority group is Turkish, descended from an Asian people who migrated from Russia and Mongolia around A.D. 900. About half the Turkish population lives in cities and half in rural areas. Kurds, the largest minority group, live in the country's mountainous regions. Arabs and whites compose smaller minorities. Nearly all the population is Sunni Muslim. The changing status of women and the extent of Islamic influence on daily life are key issues in Turkish society.

Economy and the Land. More than half the workers in this developing country are farmers, but industrialization has increased greatly since 1950. The most productive lands are in the mild coastal regions, although wheat and barley are grown in the desertlike plateau area. The government owns or controls many important industries, transportation services, and utilities, while most small farms and manufacturing companies are privately owned.

History and Politics. Hittites began to migrate to the area from Europe or central Asia around 2000 B.C. Successive dominant groups included Phrygians, Greeks, Persians, and Romans. Muslims and Christians battled in the area during the Crusades of the eleventh and twelfth centuries. In the 1300s Ottoman Turks began to build what would become a vast empire. The Republic of Turkey was founded by Mustafa Kemal in 1923, after the collapse of the six-hundred-year-old Ottoman Empire. In 1960 the Turkish government was overthrown by Turkish military forces, who subsequently set up a provisional government, adopted a new constitution, and held free elections. In the sixties and seventies disputes with Greece over Cyprus, populated by majority Greeks and minority Turks, flared into violence, and radical groups committed terrorist acts against the government, which changed hands several times. Turkey's generals assumed power in 1980 and restored order to the country. The government returned to civilian rule in 1983. ∎

UNITED KINGDOM

Official name United Kingdom of Great Britain and Northern Ireland

PEOPLE
Population 56,040,000. **Density** 596/mi² (230/km²). **Urban** 76%. **Capital** London, England, 6,851,400. **Ethnic groups** English 81%, Scottish 10%, Irish 2%, Welsh 2%, Ulster 2%. **Languages** English. **Religions** Anglican, Roman Catholic, Presbyterian. **Life expectancy** 76 female, 72 male. **Literacy** 99%.

POLITICS
Government Constitutional monarchy. **Parties** Conservative, Labor, Liberal, Social Democratic. **Suffrage** Universal, over 18. **Memberships** CW, NATO, OECD, UN. **Subdivisions** 54 counties in England and Wales, 12 regions in Scotland and island areas, 26 districts in Northern Ireland.

ECONOMY
GNP $482,700,000,000. **Per capita** $8,620. **Monetary unit** Pound sterling. **Trade partners** U.S., West Germany, other Western European countries. **Exports** Machinery, transportation equipment, petroleum, manufactured goods. **Imports** Machinery, food, crude materials, manufactured goods.

LAND
Description Northwestern European islands. **Area** 94,092 mi² (243,694 km²). **Highest point** Ben Nevis, Scotland, 4,406 ft (1,343 m). **Lowest point** Holme Fen, England, 9 ft (3 m) below sea level.

People. The ancestry of modern Britons reflects many centuries of invasions and migrations from Scandinavia and the European continent. Today Britons are a mixture of Celtic, Roman, Anglo-Saxon, Norse, and Norman influences. English is the official language, although Celtic languages such as Welsh and Scottish Gaelic are also spoken. Anglican is the dominant religion in England, while many Scots practice Presbyterianism. A sizable minority is Roman Catholic. The population is primarily urban and suburban.

Economy and the Land. A land of limited natural resources, the United Kingdom has relied on trading and, more recently, manufacturing to achieve its stature as a world power. Access to the sea is a traditional economic and political asset: the country maintains a large merchant fleet, which at one time dominated world trade. The industrial revolution developed quickly in Great Britain, and the country continues to be a leading producer of transportation equipment, metal products, and other manufactured goods. Agriculture is hindered by climate and limited suitable land, but intensive, mechanized farming methods have allowed the nation to produce half of its food supply. Livestock raising is especially important. Extensive deposits of coal and iron ore make mining important and have contributed to industry. London maintains its position as an international financial center. The United Kingdom includes Scotland, England, Wales, Northern Ireland, and several offshore islands. The varied terrain is marked by several mountain ranges, moors, rolling hills, and plains. The climate is tempered by proximity to the sea but is subject to frequent changes. Great Britain administers many overseas possessions.

History and Politics. Little is known of the earliest inhabitants of Britain, but evidence such as Stonehenge indicates the existence of a developed culture before the Roman invasion in the 50s B.C. Britain began to interact with the rest of Europe while under Roman rule, and the Norman period after A.D. 1066 fostered the establishment of many cultural and political traditions that continue to be reflected in British life. Scotland came under the British Crown in 1603, and in 1707 England and Scotland agreed to unite as Great Britain. Ireland had been conquered by the early seventeenth century, and the 1801 British Act of Union established the United Kingdom of Great Britain and Ireland. Colonial and economic expansion had taken Great Britain to the Far East, America, Africa, and India, but the nation's influence began to diminish at the end of the nineteenth century as the industrial revolution strengthened other nations. World War I significantly weakened the United Kingdom, and after the war the British Empire lost several components, including southern Ireland in 1921. The period following World War II saw the demise of the empire, with many former colonies gaining independence. ∎

VATICAN CITY

Official name State of the Vatican City
PEOPLE
Population 700. **Density** 3,500/mi² (1,750/km²). **Urban** 100%. **Capital** Vatican City, 700. **Ethnic groups** Italian. **Languages** Italian, Latin. **Religions** Roman Catholic. **Literacy** 100%.
POLITICS
Government Ecclesiastical state. **Parties** None. **Suffrage** Roman Catholic cardinals less than 80 years old. **Memberships** None. **Subdivisions** None.
ECONOMY
Monetary unit Italian lira.
LAND
Description Southern Europe, landlocked (within the city of Rome, Italy). **Area** 0.2 mi² (0.4 km²). **Highest point** 245 ft (75 m). **Lowest point** 62 ft (19 m).

People. The Vatican City, the smallest independent state in the world, is the administrative and spiritual center of the Roman Catholic church and home to the pope, the church's head. The population is composed of administrative and diplomatic workers of more than a dozen nationalities; Italians and Swiss predominate. A military corps known as the Swiss Guard is also in residence. Roman Catholicism is the only religion. The official language is Italian, although official acts of the Holy See are drawn up in Latin.

Economy and the Land. The Vatican City does not engage in commerce per se; however, it does issue its own coins and postage stamps. In addition, it is the destination of thousands of tourists and pilgrims each year. Lying on a hill west of the Tiber River, the Vatican City is an urban enclave in northwestern Rome, Italy. The Vatican City enjoys a mild climate moderated by the Mediterranean Sea.

History and Politics. For centuries the popes of the Roman Catholic church ruled the Papal States, an area across central Italy, which included Rome. The popes' temporal authority gradually was reduced to the city of Rome, which itself was eventually annexed by the Kingdom of Italy in 1870. Denying these rulings, the pope declared himself a prisoner in the Vatican, a status that lasted fifty-nine years. The Vatican City has been an independent sovereign state since 1929, when Italy signed the Treaty of the Lateran in return for papal dissolution of the Papal States. The pope heads all branches of government, though day-to-day responsibilities are delegated to staff members. ∎

YUGOSLAVIA

Official name Socialist Federal Republic of Yugoslavia
PEOPLE
Population 23,075,000. **Density** 234/mi² (90/km²). **Urban** 39%. **Capital** Belgrade, 936,200. **Ethnic groups** Serb 36%, Croatian 20%, Bosnian 9%, Slovene 8%, Albanian 8%, Macedonian 6%, Montenegrin 3%, Hungarian 2%. **Languages** Serbo-Croatian, Slovene, Macedonian. **Religions** Serbian Orthodox 41%, Roman Catholic 32%, Muslim 12%. **Life expectancy** 73 female, 69 male. **Literacy** 85%.
POLITICS
Government Socialist republic. **Parties** League of Communists. **Suffrage** Universal, over 18. **Memberships** OECD, UN. **Subdivisions** 6 republics, 2 autonomous provinces.
ECONOMY
GNP $53,900,000,000. **Per capita** $2,370. **Monetary unit** Dinar. **Trade partners** U.S.S.R., West Germany, Italy, U.S., Czechoslovakia. **Exports** Food, leather goods and shoes, machinery, textiles, wood products. **Imports** Machinery, petroleum, iron and steel, chemicals.
LAND
Description Eastern Europe. **Area** 98,766 mi² (255,804 km²). **Highest point** Triglav, 9,393 ft (2,863 m). **Lowest point** Sea level.

People. The population of Yugoslavia is one of the most diverse in Eastern Europe, composed of nearly twenty distinct ethnic groups in addition to the main Serbian and Croatian groups. Serbo-Croatian, Slovene, and Macedonian are major languages, and religions are diverse as well, often dividing along ethnic lines. Most Yugoslavs work in industry, resulting in a steady urban shift since World War II and a corresponding rise in the standard of living.

Economy and the Land. Since 1945 Yugoslavia's economy has made a successful transition from agriculture to industry. Once modeled on that of the Soviet Union, the economy today is somewhat decentralized, based on the theory of workers' self-management. Decisions on production, prices, and income are made to benefit society as a whole, though wealth has tended to concentrate in the highly industrialized north, resulting in increasing social tension. Agriculture also plays a part in the economic picture, and farming is helped by the moderate climate along the coast of the Adriatic Sea, with stronger seasonal variations in the mountainous inland regions.

History and Politics. Yugoslavia has been inhabited for at least 100,000 years, its peoples including Illyrians, Thracians, Greeks, Celts, and Romans. In A.D. 395 the Roman Empire was divided into the West Roman Empire and the Byzantine Empire, with the dividing line through present-day Yugoslavia. People in the western region became Roman Catholic and used the Roman alphabet, while Byzantines adopted the Eastern Orthodox faith and the Cyrillic alphabet. Slavic migrations led to the establishment of independent Slavic states such as Serbia and Croatia, and calls for Slavic unity began in the early 1800s. In 1914 a Slavic patriot assassinated Archduke Ferdinand of Austria-Hungary and triggered World War I. The Kingdom of Serbs, Croats, and Slovenes was formed in 1918, but infighting encouraged King Alexander I to declare himself dictator in 1929 and change the new country's name to Yugoslavia, which was retained after Alexander's assassination in 1934. Germany and the other Axis powers invaded Yugoslavia during World War II and were opposed by a partisan army organized by Josip Broz Tito, who assumed leadership when Yugoslavia became a Communist republic in 1945. Tito's policy of nonalignment, the cornerstone of Yugoslavia's foreign policy, caused Russia to break off diplomatic relations from 1948 to 1955. United States aid from the 1940s to the 1960s encouraged a shift toward Western trade and broadened political and cultural exchanges as well. Tito's course of independence and interaction with non-aligned nations continued after his death in 1980. ■

World Facts & Comparisons

General Information

Equatorial circumference of the earth, 24,901.45 miles
Polar circumference of the earth, 24,855.33
Total area of the earth, 197,000,000 square miles
Highest elevation on the earth's surface, Mt. Everest, Asia, 29,028
Lowest elevation on the earth's surface, shores of the Dead Sea,
   Asia — 1,312 feet below sea level
Greatest known depth of the ocean, south of the Mariana Islands,
   Pacific Ocean, 35,810 feet

Area of Africa, 11,700,000 square miles
Area of Antarctica, 5,400,000 square miles
Area of Asia, 17,300,000 square miles
Area of Europe, 3,800,000 square miles
Area of North America, 9,400,000 square miles
Area of Oceania, incl. Australia, 3,300,000 square miles
Area of South America, 6,900,000 square miles
Population of the earth (est. 1/1/87), 4,975,000,000

Principal Islands and Their Areas

ISLAND Country   Area (Sq. Mi.)

Baffin I., Canada 195,928
Banks I., Canada 27,038
Borneo (Kalimantan), Asia 258,855
Bougainville, Papua New Guinea . . . 3,880
Celebes (Sulawesi), Indonesia 73,057
Corsica, France 3,352
Crete, Greece 3,189
Cuba, North America 40,519
Cyprus, Asia 3,572
Devon I., Canada 21,331
Ellesmere I., Canada 83,896
Great Britain, United Kingdom . . . 88,795
Greenland, North America 840,004
Hainan I., China 13,127
Hawaii, United States 4,021
Hispaniola, North America 29,418
Hokkaidō, Japan 30,088
Honshū, Japan 87,804
Iceland, Europe 39,769

Ireland, Europe 32,588
Jamaica, North America 4,244
Java (Jawa), Indonesia 51,038
Kyūshū, Japan 14,154
Luzon, Philippines 40,420
Madagascar, Africa 226,658
Melville I., Canada 16,274
Mindanao, Philippines 36,537
New Britain, Papua New Guinea . . 14,592
New Caledonia, Oceania 5,671
Newfoundland, Canada 43,359
New Guinea, Indonesia-Papua New
   Guinea 303,090
North East Land, Norway 6,350
North I., New Zealand 44,297
Novaya Zemlya (N. part), Soviet
   Union 18,882
Prince of Wales I., Canada 12,872
Puerto Rico, North America 3,515

Sakhalin, Soviet Union 29,498
Sardinia, Italy 9,301
Shikoku, Japan 7,053
Sicily, Italy 9,926
Somerset I., Canada 9,570
Southampton I., Canada 15,913
South I., New Zealand 58,093
Spitsbergen, Norway 15,260
Sri Lanka, Asia 24,962
Sumatra (Sumatera) . . Indonesia . . 182,860
Taiwan, Asia 13,885
Tasmania, Australia 26,383
Tierra del Fuego, Isla Grande
   de South America, ... 18,600
Timor, Indonesia 13,094
Vancouver I., Canada 12,079
Victoria I., Canada 75,767

Principal Lakes, Oceans, Seas and Their Areas

LAKE Country   Area (Sq. Mi.)

Arabian Sea, ... 1,492,000
Aral Sea, Soviet Union (salt) . . . 24,750
Arctic Ocean, ... 5,400,000
Atlantic Ocean, ... 31,800,000
Baikal, L., Soviet Union 12,160
Balkhash, L., Soviet Union 7,065
Baltic Sea, Europe 163,000
Bengal, Bay of, Asia 839,000
Bering Sea, ... 876,000
Black Sea, ... 178,000
Caribbean Sea, ... 1,063,000
Caspian Sea, Iran-Soviet Union
   (salt) 143,240
Chad, L., Cameroon-Chad-Nigeria . . 6,300
East China Sea, Asia 482,000
Erie, L., Canada-United States 9,910
Eyre, L., Australia (salt) 3,668

Great Bear Lake, Canada 12,028
Great Slave Lake, Canada 11,031
Greenland Sea, ... 465,000
Hudson Bay, Canada 475,000
Huron, L., Canada-United States . . 23,000
Indian Ocean, ... 28,900,000
Japan, Sea of, Asia 389,000
Ladoga, L., Soviet Union 6,835
Mai-Ndombe, Lac, Zaire 3,100
Mediterranean Sea, ... , . . 967,000
Mexico, Gulf of, North America . . 596,000
Michigan, L., United States 22,300
Nicaragua, Lago de, Nicaragua . . . 3,150
North Sea, Europe 222,000
Norwegian Sea, Europe 597,000
Nyasa,
   L., Malawi-Mozambique-Tanzania . 11,150

Okhotsk, Sea of, Asia 619,000
Onega, L., Soviet Union 3,750
Ontario, L., Canada-United States . . 7,540
Pacific Ocean, ... 63,800,000
Red Sea, ... 169,000
South China Sea, Asia 1,331,000
Superior, L., Canada-United
   States 31,700
Tanganyika, L.,
   Burundi-Tanzania-Zaire-Zambia . 12,350
Titicaca, Lago, Bolivia-Peru 3,200
Victoria,
   L., Kenya-Tanzania-Uganda 26,820
Winnipeg, L., Canada 9,417
Yellow Sea, Asia 480,000

Principal Mountains and Their Heights

MOUNTAIN Country   Elev. (Ft.)

Aconcagua, Cerro, Argentina 22,831
Annapurna, Nepal 26,504
Apo, Mt., Philippines 9,692
Ararat, Mt., Turkey 16,804
Barre des Écrins, France 13,458
Barú, Volcán, Panama 11,411
Belukha, Mt., Soviet Union 14,783
Blanc, Mont (Monte
   Bianco), France-Italy 15,771

Bolívar, Pico, Venezuela 16,427
Bonete, Cerro, Argentina 22,546
Borah Pk., Idaho 12,662
Cameroon, Mont, Cameroon 13,353
Carrauntoohil, Ireland 3,406
Chimborazo, Ecuador 20,702
Chirripó, Cerro, Costa Rica 12,533
Citlaltépetl, Volcán, Mexico 18,701
Communism Pk., Soviet Union 24,590

Cook, Mt., New Zealand 12,349
Cotopaxi, Ecuador 19,347
Cristóbal Colón, Pico, Colombia . . . 19,029
Demavend, Mt., Iran 18,386
Dhaulāgiri, Nepal 26,810
Dykh-Tau, Mt., Soviet Union 17,073
Elbert, Mt., Colorado 14,433
Elbrus, Mt., Soviet Union 18,510
Estrela, Portugal (continental) 6,539

MOUNTAIN Country	Elev. (Ft.)
Etna, Mt., Italy	10,902
Everest, Mt., China-Nepal	29,028
Finsteraarhorn, Switzerland	14,022
Fitzroy, Monte (Cerro Chaltel) Argentina-Chile	11,073
Fuji, Mt., Japan	12,388
Gasherbrum, China-Pakistan	26,470
Gerlachovka, Czechoslovakia	8,711
Glittertinden, Norway	8,110
Gongga Mtn. (Minya Konka), China	24,790
Grand Teton, Wyoming	13,770
Grossglockner, Austria	12,457
Gunnbjoørn Fjeld, Greenland	12,139
Haltia, Finland-Norway	4,357
Hkakabo Razi, Burma	19,296
Hood, Mt., Oregon	11,235
Huascarán, Nevado, Peru	22,123
Huila, Nevado del, Colombia	18,865
Hvannadalshnúkur, Iceland	6,952
Illampu, Nevado, Bolivia	20,873
Ixtacihuatl, Mexico	17,343
Jaya Pk., Indonesia	16,503
Jungfrau, Switzerland	13,642
K2 (Godwin Austen), China-Pakistan	28,250
Kämet, China-India	25,447
Känchenjunga, Nepal-India	28,208
Kangrinboqê Mtn., China	22,028
Karisimbi, Volcan, Rwanda-Zaire	14,787
Kebnekaise, Sweden	6,926
Kilimanjaro, Tanzania	19,340
Kinabalu, Mt., Malaysia	13,432
Kirinyaga (Mt. Kenya), Kenya	17,058

Kirkpatrick, Mt., Antarctica	14,856
Korab, Albania-Yugoslavia	9,026
Kosciusko, Mt., Australia	7,310
Koussi, Emi, Chad	11,204
Kula Kangri, Bhutan	24,784
Lassen Pk., California	10,457
Lenin Pk., Soviet Union	23,406
Llullaillaco, Volcán, Argentina-Chile	22,110
Logan, Mt., Canada	19,524
McKinley, Mt., Alaska	20,320
Makälu, China-Nepal	27,825
Margherita Pk., Zaire-Uganda	16,763
Markham, Mt., Antarctica	14,275
Matterhorn, Italy-Switzerland	14,692
Mauna Kea, Hawaii	13,796
Mauna Loa, Hawaii	13,679
Meru, Mt., Tanzania	14,978
Misti, Volcán, Peru	19,101
Moldoveanu, Romania	8,343
Mulhacén, Spain	11,411
Musala, Bulgaria	9,596
Muztag, China	25,338
Muztagata, China	24,757
Nabi Shuayb, Mt., Yemen	12,336
Namcha Barwa, China	25,446
Nanda Devi, India	25,645
Nånga Parbat, Pakistan	26,660
Narodnaya, Mt., Soviet Union	6,217
Neblina, Pico da, Brazil-Venezuela	9,888
Nevis, Ben, United Kingdom	4,406
Nowshãk, Afghanistan-Pakistan	24,557
Ojos del Salado, Nevado, Argentina-Chile	22,572

Ólimbos, Cyprus	6,401
Olympus, Mt., Greece	9,570
Paricutín, Mexico	9,213
Pico, Ponta do, Portugal	7,713
Pikes Pk., Colorado	14,110
Pobedy, Pk., China-Soviet Union	24,406
Popocatépetl, Volcán, Mexico	17,887
Rainier, Mt., Washington	14,410
Ras Dashen Terara, Ethiopia	15,158
Rosa, Monte (Dufourspitze), Italy-Switzerland	15,203
Rysy, Czechoslovakia-Poland	8,199
St. Elias, Mt., Alaska-Canada	18,008
Sajama, Nevado, Bolivia	21,463
Shasta, Mt., California	14,162
Shkhara, Mt., Soviet Union	16,627
Tajumulco, Volcán, Guatemala	13,846
Teide, Pico de, Spain	12,198
Tirich Mïr, Pakistan	25,230
Triglav, Yugoslavia	9,393
Trikora Pk., Indonesia	15,584
Vesuvius, Italy	4,190
Vinson Massif, Antarctica	16,864
Viso, Mt., Italy	12,602
Weisshorn, Switzerland	14,780
Whitney, Mt., California	14,494
Wilhelm, Mt., Papua New Guinea	14,793
Wrangell, Mt., Alaska	14,163
Xixabangma Mtn. (Gosainthan), China	26,286
Yerupaja, Nevado, Peru	21,765
Yü, Mt., Taiwan	13,114
Zugspitze, Austria-Germany, Fed. Rep. of	9,716

Principal Rivers and Their Lengths

RIVER Continent	Length (Mi.)
Aldan, Asia	1,412
Amazon-Ucayali, South America	4,000
Amu Darya, Asia	1,578
Amur-Argun, Asia	2,761
Angara, Asia	1,105
Araguaia, South America	1,367
Arkansas, North America	1,459
Brahmaputra, Asia	1,770
Brazos, North America	870
Canadian, North America	906
Churchill, North America	1,000
Colorado, North America (U.S.-Mexico)	1,450
Colorado, North America (Texas)	840
Columbia, North America	1,243
Congo (Zaïre), Africa	2,900
Danube, Europe	1,776
Darling, Australia	864
Dnepr, Europe	1,368
Dnestr, Europe	840
Don, Europe	1,162
Elbe (Labe), Europe	720
Euphrates (Fiırat), Asia	1,510
Fraser, North America	850
Ganges, Asia	1,560
Godävari, Asia	930
Grande, Rio, North America	1,885
Huang He (Yellow), Asia	3,395
Indus, Asia	1,800
Irrawaddy, Asia	1,238
Juruá, South America	1,250
Kama, Europe	1,122

Kasai (Cassai), Africa	1,338
Kolyma, Asia	1,323
Lena, Asia	2,734
Limpopo, Africa	1,100
Loire, Europe	625
Mackenzie, North America	2,635
Madeira-Mamoré, South America	1,988
Magdalena, South America	950
Marañón, South America	1,000
Mekong, Asia	2,600
Mississippi, North America	2,348
Mississippi-Missouri, North America	3,740
Missouri, North America	2,315
Murray, Australia	1,566
Murray-Darling, Australia	2,330
Negro, South America	1,305
Nemunas (Neman), Europe	582
Niger, Africa	2,600
Nile-Kagera, Africa	4,145
Northern Donets, Europe	735
Ob, Asia	2,287
Ob-Irtysh, Asia	3,362
Oder (Odra), Europe	565
Ohio, North America	981
Oka, Europe	932
Orange, Africa	1,300
Orinoco, South America	1,600
Paraguay (Paraguai), South America	1,610
Paraná, South America	2,796
Peace, North America	1,195
Pechora, Europe	1,124

Pilcomayo, South America	1,550
Purús, South America	1,860
Red, North America	1,270
Rhine, Europe	820
Rio de la Plata-Paraná, South America	3,030
Roosevelt, South America	950
Saint Lawrence, North America	800
Salado, South America	870
Salween (Nu Jiang), Asia	1,750
São Francisco, South America	1,988
Saskatchewan-Bow, North America	1,205
Snake, North America	1,038
Syr Darya, Asia	1,876
Tagus (Tejo) (Tajo), Europe	625
Tarim He, Asia	1,328
Tennessee, North America	652
Tigris (Dıicle), Asia	1,180
Tisza (Tisa), Europe	607
Tocantins, South America	1,640
Ucayali, South America	1,220
Ural, Asia	1,509
Uruguay (Uruguai), South America	1,025
Vilyuy, Asia	1,647
Volga, Europe	2,194
Wisła (Vistula), Europe	630
Xingu, South America	1,230
Yangtze (Chang Jiang), Asia	3,915
Yenisey, Asia	2,543
Yukon, North America	1,979
Zambezi, Africa	1,700

INDEX

Introduction to the Index

This index includes in a single alphabetical list the names of many important features shown on the maps. Each name is followed by a location reference, a map-reference key, and a page number.

The names of physical features appear in the index followed by terms to indicate their nature—b. for bay, r. for river, mtn. for mountain, etc. The names of physical features are listed under the proper, not the generic, part of the name. For example, "Mount Etna" appears in the index as "Etna, Mount."

Country designations follow the names of most places in the index. The locations of places in the United Kingdom are defined by abbreviations that indicate the political division in which each is located. Names of continents follow features that extend beyond the boundaries of one country.

Each map-reference key consists of a letter and a number. The letters appear along the sides of the maps. A lower-case letter indicates reference to an inset. The numbers appear across the tops and bottoms of the maps. Page numbers for two-page maps always refer to left-hand pages only.

Abbreviations used in the index are listed below.

List of Abbreviations

Alb.	Albania	hist. reg.	historic region	Pol.	Poland
And.	Andorra	Hung.	Hungary	Port.	Portugal
Aus.	Austria	i.	island	r.	river
b.	bay, gulf	Ice.	Iceland	reg.	physical region
Bel.	Belgium	ice	ice feature, glacier	res.	reservoir
Bul.	Bulgaria	I. of Man	Isle of Man	Rom.	Romania
c.	cape, point	Ire.	Ireland	Scot., U.K.	Scotland, U.K.
ctry.	independent country	is.	islands	Sov. Un.	Soviet Union
Czech.	Czechoslovakia	l.	lake, pond	state	state, republic, canton
Den.	Denmark	Liech.	Liechtenstein		
dep.	dependency, colony	Lux.	Luxembourg	strt.	strait, channel, sound
Eng., U.K.	England, U.K.	mth.	river mouth or channel		
est.	estuary			sw.	swamp, marsh
Eur.	Europe	mtn.	mountain	Swe.	Sweden
Fin.	Finland	mts.	mountains	Switz.	Switzerland
for.	forest, moor	Neth.	Netherlands	ter.	territory
Fr.	France	N. Ire., U.K.	Northern Ireland, U.K.	Tur.	Turkey
F.R.Ger.	Federal Republic of Germany			U.K.	United Kingdom
		Nor.	Norway	val.	valley, watercourse
Ger.D.R.	German Democratic Republic	pen.	peninsula	vol.	volcano
		pl.	plain, flat	Wales, U.K.	Wales, U.K.
Grc.	Greece	plat.	plateau, highland	Yugo.	Yugoslavia
hist.	historic site, ruins				

A

Name	Map Ref	Page
Aachen, F.R.Ger.	C3	40
Aalen, F.R.Ger.	D5	40
Aalst (Alost), Bel.	B6	38
Aare, r., Switz.	E3	40
Aberdare, Wales, U.K.	E5	36
Aberdeen, Scot., U.K.	B5	36
Acqui [Terme], Italy	B2	42
Adige, r., Italy	B3	42
Adriatic Sea, Eur.	G10	34
Aegean Sea	C5	54
Ahlen, F.R.Ger.	C3	40
Ahvenanmaa (Åland), is., Fin.	G9	50
Aix-en-Provence, Fr.	F6	42
Ajaccio, Fr.	D2	42
Akranes, Ice.	n21	50
Akureyri, Ice.	n23	50
Åland, see Ahvenanmaa, is., Fin.	G9	50
Albacete, Spain	C5	46
Alba Iulia, Rom.	B6	48

Name	Map Ref	Page
Albania, ctry., Eur.	B2	54
Albano Laziale, Italy	D4	42
Alborán, i., Spain	E4	46
Ålborg, Den.	I3	50
Alcalá [de Guadaira], Spain	D3	46
Alcalá de Henares, Spain	B4	46
Alcamo, Italy	F4	42
Alcázar de San Juan, Spain	C4	46
Alcira, Spain	C5	46
Alcobendas, Spain	o17	46
Alcorcón, Spain	p17	46
Alcoy, Spain	C5	46
Aldershot, Eng., U.K.	E6	36
Alessandria, Italy	B2	42
Ålesund, Nor.	F2	50
Alexandria, Rom.	D7	48
Algarve, hist. reg., Port.	D1	46
Algeciras, Spain	D3	46
Algorta (Guecho), Spain	A4	46
Alicante, Spain	C5	46

Name	Map Ref	Page
Alingsås, Swe.	I5	50
Alkmaar, Neth.	A6	38
Allenstein, see Olsztyn, Pol.	B6	44
Aller, r., Eur.	B4	40
Almada, Port.	C1	46
Almelo, Neth.	A7	38
Almería, Spain	D4	46
Alps, mts., Eur.	E4	40
Alsace, hist. reg., Fr.	C7	38
Altamura, Italy	D6	42
Altenburg, Ger.D.R.	C6	40
Alverca, Port.	f9	46
Amersfoort, Neth.	A6	38
Amiens, Fr.	C5	38
Amsterdam, Neth.	A6	38
Ancona, Italy	C4	42
Andalusia, hist. reg., Spain	D3	46
Anderlecht, Bel.	B6	38
Andorra, And.	A6	46